To Paul Larson –
with affectionate
good wishes as
he goes to teaching.

G. M. P. Frann

Summer 1975.

— auto trials - system
terrible. 74

— divorce - 110

AMERICAN LAW:
The Case for Radical Reform

Other Books by John P. Frank

Mr. Justice Black (1949)
Cases on Constitutional Law (1950)
Cases on the Constitution (1951)
My Son's Story (1952)
Marble Palace (1958)
Lincoln as a Lawyer (1961)
Justice Daniel Dissenting (1964)
The Warren Court (1964)

LECTURES BY

John P. Frank

UPON THE DEDICATION OF
The Earl Warren Legal Center
UNIVERSITY OF CALIFORNIA

AMERICAN LAW:
The Case for Radical Reform

THE MACMILLAN COMPANY
COLLIER-MACMILLAN LIMITED LONDON

Library of Congress Catalog Card Number: 70-88839

First Printing

THE MACMILLAN COMPANY
COLLIER-MACMILLAN CANADA LIMITED, TORONTO, ONTARIO

Printed in the United States of America

To
CHIEF JUSTICE EARL WARREN
A GREAT JUDICIAL ADMINISTRATOR

Contents

Preface

Some two hundred years ago Horace Walpole predicted that "the next Augustan Age will dawn on the other side of the Atlantic." His reputation as a prophet may prove to be good whether one relates his statement to the earlier excesses of the Roman Emperor or to his later grandeur. The answer remains with us. If we bear in mind the admonition that Thomas Carlyle gave his English brethren in 1843 that "we [the English] have more riches than any other nation. . . . [But] we have less good"; or if we remember the teachings of the satirical pen of Charles Dickens in "Bleak House" ten years later; or if we practice the theory of positive justice rather than negative freedom that Thomas Hill Green posited a score of years thereafter; or if we take heed of the revealing exposures of the "injustices of justice" of John Galsworthy in the first decade of the twentieth century; or if we but hear the plaintive pleas of the shoemaker and his fellow inmate, the fish peddler—Sacco and Vanzetti, in their "Letters from Prison"—we may well surpass the record of the great Augustus.

Our problem seems to be our propensity to overlook the overtures of history. Thomas Jefferson was one of the first to sense this weakness. He wisely advised us that "the execution of the laws is more important than the making of them." This warning, however, fell on deaf ears. Even in the constitutional field we have failed miserably.

Although the Bill of Rights was included in the Constitution by ratification as early as 1791, some of the Amendments—especially IV, V, VI, and VII—are not enjoyed by all of our citizens today. And I daresay that "the wall of separation" between church and state built into the First Amendment is recognized in the breach. Likewise the collision of fair trial and free press in the everyday life of our people often results in a total destruction of one or the other. Although the Fourteenth Amendment is now in its 101st year, many of the fruits of its clauses are not enjoyed by millions of our citizens. Indeed, the news media report every day of the many anguished cries that call for equal justice. Many of our communities have of late experienced bloody and destructive riots that some attribute to the laissez faire attitude of most of us. Only last year our capital city was caught up in such a debacle within a few blocks of the very heart of our national government. And only last summer we saw a wagon train filled with the poor and the dissatisfied move through the South dramatizing the plight of Negro citizens and, upon reaching Washington, pour its cargo into "Resurrection City," which they erected within the very shadow of the Washington Monument. And what did we do about these things? Pitifully little! Indeed, in some cities we have not yet cleaned up the debris!

Now our institutes of higher education—the citadels of our liberties—have been caught up in the milieu. Many of their halls have been forcibly seized and held in defiance of constituted authority. And at least one was turned into an armed camp of insurrectionists demanding a pound of flesh from the authorities and amnesty as well. And what have we done about this? In most instances, condoned it!

Prosecutions have been instituted following some of the riots. However, even in our capital city most of these cases have not yet come to trial. How can we expect to cope with these recurring situations unless our court machinery moves more swiftly and with effectiveness? Sure and undelayed punishment for those who offend the law is the greatest of all deterrents. In the college area I know of but one instance where the law's sanctions were even sought, much less recognized. Furthermore, I find nothing in the law that permits anyone to forgive its penalties regardless of the truth of their motives or the justness of their cause. This is not to say, however, that we must not afford effective sanction for those who are deprived of justice and cry out for it. We must move just as swiftly to afford them redemption.

The truth about it is that we are sadly deficient in the area that John Galsworthy calls "the injustices of justice." Just recently I received a copy of a Report on the Administration of Criminal Justice in a Southwestern city. Climaxing an investigation of several months, the report—issued about a year ago—is one of the most revealing ever brought to my attention. One of its findings was "that those officials who are charged with the responsibility of enforcing the law do not accept their own obligation to obey the law." This is a most serious charge. I would be prone to discount it but for its documentation. Among the injustices uncovered are the following:

> "Investigative arrests" under which police officers arrest persons without a warrant and hold them for investigation from five to eight days without booking, without bail, and without counsel. These prisoners are confined in maximum security cells that have double-decker beds without mattresses. If one has funds and is lucky, he may be able to get word out to his counsel and get "sprung" by filing a *habeas corpus*. Prisoners held for city offenses are held in large "tanks" that are rectangular rooms with bars on the hall side and walls on the other three, along which are "hard benches" on which prisoners may sit or sleep. There are no beds. From twenty-five to seventy-five men are confined here at one time. The room has a single open toilet. The floor, though cleaned once a day, becomes "covered with urine, feces and vomit." Each twenty-four hours court is opened in a police assembly room in the basement of the jail. Those pris-

oners in the "tank," who have not previously been taken before the judge, are chained together, led to the assembly room, and permitted to plead. Those pleading guilty and who are fined but cannot pay are required to serve out their sentence at the rate of $5 credit for each day.

Attorneys act as bondsmen as well as counsel, charging for both services. The going rate is 15 percent of the face of the bond.

Warrants, when sought by the police, are secured on a form affidavit forwarded to a Justice of the Peace. The latter's clerk issues it as a matter of course without reference to the Justice.

When examining trials are held the prisoner is not advised fully of his rights but is always remanded to the Grand Jury without fixing bail or appointing counsel. His only recourse, if he has funds, is to secure his own counsel and file an application for habeas corpus. If he is too poor to do this, he remains in jail.

The District Attorney decides when an arraignment will be held, when counsel will be appointed, and when the case will be tried.

Bail, if granted pending trial, is usually set at the amount suggested by the District Attorney. Poor defendants remain in jail.

There is no criminal legal aid office or public defender system. Appointment of counsel for indigent defendants usually depends upon what lawyers are in the courtroom or in the hallway when the arraignment is held. At times the judge refers to a list of young inexperienced attorneys. "In a large number of cases" the prosecutor suggests who should be appointed as counsel.

Guilty pleas are obtained in felony cases by the use of a "cop-out man" who officially is an investigator of the District Attorney. In misdemeanor cases the prisoners are brought before the Court chained together and given an opportunity to plead without warning, arraignment, or counsel. The defendant in misdemeanor cases is denied counsel at every stage save the final one.

If counsel is requested by a prisoner, he is assured that he is entitled to one and will get him "a little later." That sometimes never comes. During the police stages of the procedure, counsel is never available.

Where counsel is appointed, the prisoner is not notified and often never hears from his counsel until the actual day of the trial.

The folklore of law enforcement existing during the early days of Texas deals with "The Law West of the Pecos" as administered by none other than Judge Roy Bean! He is reputed to have always given the defendant a trial—and then hanged him. The system as outlined in this Report is somewhat reminiscent. It is to be hoped that there are no other comparable situations among our municipalities. However, the chances are that there are many. In addition, we do know that the small claims courts of the country are woefully inadequate. Rather than being a haven for those without funds, they are a yoke of oppression and abuse. Finally, our courts of general jurisdiction in metropolitan areas are struggling under tremendous case backlogs.

These situations are a disgrace to our judicature. They only illustrate that our efforts of the last score of years to modernize our courts and to make more effective their procedures have been far too little and too late. We have made some progress in the federal field, beginning with Chief Justice Taft's success in the creation in 1922 of what we now call the Judicial Conference of the United States. It was also Taft who "lobbied" through the Judges Bill in 1927 that has enabled the Supreme Court to keep abreast of its docket. Moreover, the adoption of the federal rules has been a monumental step forward. This was made possible in 1958 through the passage of the Judicial Conference Rules of Practice and Procedure Act, Public Law 85-513, 72 Stat. 356, which authorizes a continuing surveillance and updating of the rules.

We have also been blessed by some stars on the state side of the judicial firmament, notably Arthur T. Vanderbilt and John J. Parker. And their good work has been supplemented by the excellent service of the Conference of State Trial Judges and the College which they have established and now operate. But as much improvement as these agencies have been able to produce, it is not enough. Moreover, as Chief Justice Taft told us almost half a century ago, "the mere increase of courts or judges will not suffice. We must have machinery of a quasi-executive character to mass our judicial force . . . we must have teamwork." In addition we must purge our existing procedures of their injustices and illegalities.

Of the many proposals that have been offered to meet this crisis, the one that strikes my fancy is that of Mr. Frank. He offers a "Warren Commission for American Law." Patterning it after the Marshall Plan, which was so effective in the rebuilding of Europe after World War II, Mr. Frank calls for an all-out effort "to reconstruct our own legal system." As he says: "American law most desperately needs a Marshall Plan; and to create it, we need precisely what the Secretary ordered, a period for a creative, fresh look." He points out that presently we have "a pig in the parlor" which is making a mess of our law. As Jefferson indicated, we must make the execution of the law more effective, develop techniques for accelerating its procedures, and conduct continuing education and training programs for those that work in its vineyards.

Mr. Frank's work needs no introduction. He is well and favorably known by every person in our country who is at all versed in judicial administration. A former law clerk of my brother Mr. Justice Black, a distinguished scholar and author, an effective advocate, and a most successful lawyer of over thirty years' experience, he is as well qualified to speak of the shortcomings of our judicial system and to suggest methods for its improvement as any person I know. The lesson that he teaches is that the law does not generate justice. It is but a declaration of principles that must be put into practice and given force and effectiveness through enlightened procedures and administration. As Mr. Frank points out, there is much law but little justice. Would it not be better to have more justice and less law? That, in short, is what he proposes. The quicker we get at it the sooner we will be able to give answer to Horace Walpole's prophecy that we truly have attained the grandeur of another Augustan Age.

JUSTICE TOM C. CLARK

Introduction

In his *Commentaries* Blackstone defined law by dividing it into making law, directing compliance with its requirements, and providing remedies for its breach. The remedies are of the utmost consequence; as he said, "In vain would rights be declared, in vain directed to be observed, if there were no method of recovering and asserting those rights when wrongfully withheld or invaded."

It is my thesis that this remedy function, the peaceful settlement of the disputes within society by the granting or withholding of remedies, is the most elemental function of the lawyer and the law today. We perform other services, we may perform more important services, but this is the first reason for our continuing existence.

At the present time the law and the lawyers are failing—utterly failing—to perform this function well; we are approaching the total bankruptcy of our remedy system. We have our backs to the wall, for there is not now on hand or on order any active program for avoiding this bankruptcy. Moreover, but for a handful of persons, we are making no effort to escape a legal doomsday; many of our most justly respected leaders at the bar and in the universities are like the crowd in Samson's temple a moment before he pushed the pillars, unconscious of the impending surprise and headache. For law has not been able to keep up with people or with automobiles.

Against this discouraging background stands the sturdy figure of Chief Justice Earl Warren. With complete sensitivity to the problems confronting our profession and our people, he has taken the lead both in action and in thought. It is wonderfully fitting that the University of California should create an Earl Warren Legal Center from which, it is devoutly hoped, solutions will come. This Center may develop, in part from the many starts made in the projects of the former Chief Justice, a program to make the American legal system capable of serving the 200 to 300 million people who will occupy our land in the remainder of this century. The Center could have no higher purpose than to link the name of Earl Warren and the administration of justice with the name of Earl Warren and equal rights, Earl Warren and representative democracy, Earl Warren and fair trial.

It is a somewhat frightening satisfaction to have had the opportunity to offer the first lectures at the Earl Warren Legal Center, and thus to be associated with so glowing a name and so golden an opportunity. It is at least fitting that the lectures be dedicated to the Chief Justice, for they are the direct result of his examples and his teachings, particularly in the committee work on procedural reform and at the American Law Institute. One always knows he cares, deeply and personally, for American justice. His oft-made observation to the effect that "more judges are not enough" gives the challenge to the bar to offer other proposals; here is my tender.

These lectures are given when I have been more than thirty years in study, teaching, practice and writing about law. I have freely drawn on personal experience, and indeed have welcomed the lecture format, which permits this. If at times I seem to call for action with a somewhat strident bugle, it is from concern for a profession that has my devotion and its professionals, who have my respect.

Let me make three disclaimers to avoid misunderstanding:

(1) I said earlier that peaceful settlement of disputes is the law's most fundamental function, the first reason for its exist-

ence, but that it may not be our most important function. I do
not in fact think that it is. Settling all the auto accident disputes in the country in one year instead of, say, four would be
an immense social reform; but it is not at the same level of social importance as ending either racial discrimination or mal-
districting of Congressional seats, which have also been law jobs.
The defects of civil justice do not have to be, and are not, the
only social problem of the law to deserve attention.

(2) I am dealing here with the cost of legal services, but only
in the sense of the factors that make them excessive. I do not
reach the problem of providing legal services for those so poor
that any reasonable price is too much. Giant strides are being
taken through legal aid societies and a variety of other programs.
Those activities are not minimized by exclusion here; they are
simply outside this line of fire.

(3) My topic is court failure, and most legal work is outside
the courts altogether. Lawyers are drafting wills and trusts, ne-
gotiating and adjusting, handling financing, pension plans, and
so on. Most taxation is unaffected by court congestion. But court
failure, without being all or even most of the law, warrants this
volume of alarm.

Too many friends have responded to my requests for suggestions to make it feasible to list them all; I would be appearing
to claim honor by association. My partners have contributed
their thoughts, and Paul M. Roca, as usual, has been my editor.
Professor Fannie Klein, of New York University Law School and
the Institute of Judicial Administration, has been indispensable
for technical advice and information; and Dean Charles Joiner
of Wayne University has been a rich source of ideas and facts.
Berkeley's Professor David Louisell of the law faculty has put me
on the platform. May he be, as he deserves to be, immune to responsibility for my enthusiasms.

The lectures as given were three; for publishing and reading
convenience, they are broken into chapters, and notes have been
added. Because some time has passed since they were given, I

have substituted the most recent statistics of the Institute of Judicial Administration and the Administrator of the United States Courts, and appended a few other subsequent developments as footnotes where I could.

JOHN P. FRANK

Phoenix, Arizona, 1969

AMERICAN LAW:

The Case for Radical Reform

I

The Problem:
The Pig in the Parlor

In 1958, Chief Justice Earl Warren said:

> Interminable and unjustifiable delays in our courts are today compromising the basic legal rights of countless thousands of Americans and, imperceptibly, corroding the very foundations of government in the United States. Today, because the legal remedies of many of our people can be realized only after they have sallowed with the passage of time, they are mere forms of justice.[1]

In 1967, the Chief Justice said:

> In a century which has been characterized by growth and modernization in science, technology and economics, the legal fraternity is still living in the past. We have allowed the mainstream of progress to pass us by. . . . Our failure to act becomes alarming when a competent district judge must admit in testimony before a Senate committee that unless something new and effective is done promptly in the area of judicial research, coordination and management, the rule of law in this nation cannot endure. When justice is denied to any of our citizens because of

2

faulty administration our failure to act becomes in-
excusable.[2]

The two statements are not parallel, nor is the one a
repetition of the other. A situation so bad in 1958 that the
basic legal rights of the people were compromised had de-
generated by 1967 to the fear expressed by the head of the
American legal system that the rule of law in our country
could not endure at all. The second statement parallels an
observation by Supreme Court Justice William Brennan that
congestion in some areas threatens "an actual breakdown
in the administration of justice."[3] Professor Charles Wright,
speaking of the future of the federal courts, finds the situation "quite desperate."[4] Attorney General Ramsey Clark
emphatically agreed with his father, Justice Tom Clark, that
"the mere addition of judges and supporting personnel is not
the answer."[5] A situation bad enough in 1958 was incalculably worse by 1968.

Why incalculably? If there is a deterioration, cannot the
deterioration be calculated? Statistically, yes; but the rate
and nature of the deterioration is incalculable all the same.
Not only has the legal machinery of the country been further burdened and further exhausted between 1958 and
1968, but hope has been very nearly exhausted, too. The
arsenal of tools with which it was hoped that a better legal
system might be created, an arsenal which existed at least
in contemplation in 1958, was largely gone by 1968. I shall
turn in some detail in a few moments to this exhaustion of
reform, but it is sufficient to say for this introductory purpose that in 1958 the profession had an unplayed ace in the
hole. We have now played it, and we have lost the pot, and
we have nothing to show for it.

Less figuratively, the profession has always before had in

reserve the possibility of creating more courts and more judges. All reforms could thus be short of this ultimate reform; this was the final expedient, the big gun that could be brought to bear to batter down the wall of delay if everything else failed. This is illustrated by the best study of the 1950's, the Zeisel, Kalven, Buchholz work, *Delay in the Court,* which carefully canvassed all of the available tools and which concluded with the reassuring note that if worst came to worst, "more judges are an ultimate remedy in the simple sense that they are the one remedy for delay that is certain to work."[6]

And so the one remedy that was certain to work was tried, and it has failed, too. The number of federal district judges was increased by legislation from 197 in 1941 to 341 in 1966, most of the increase coming in the 1960's; and as will be shown statistically, the situation did not materially improve.

Let me illustrate in terms of personal experience. When I left teaching to come to the full-time practice of law in Phoenix, Arizona, in 1954, the state had two federal district judges and cases were tried as quickly as lawyers would wish them to be. Today there are four, and delays are substantial. In the state court in Phoenix, Arizona, there were at that time nine trial judges; today there are twenty-one. The docket then was current and today it is far behind.

The federal experience is particularly gloomy because such great care was taken in the choice of the new judges. This was no matter of loading the bench with favorites or incompetents. On the whole, a superb and conscientious job was done, a job in which the entire profession was involved because of the high development during this period of the method by which an American Bar Association committee recommended appointments.[7] In the main, the appointees were as good as conscientious public officials and conscientious bar leaders could find. Nonetheless, we are doing so badly that the Chief Justice of the United States warns us that the rule of law may not endure.

What the Chief Justice is telling us is that more judges are not enough. He adds:

> We have learned by sad experience that merely adding judgeships will not solve the problem of judicial administration. Indeed, adding more judges to courts using outmoded methods of administration is more likely to retard production than it is to stimulate it.[8]

Justice Tom Clark, the country's most distinguished expert on state judicial administration, says the same thing: "Generally, however, we do not need more judges. We discovered that in the federal system."[9] Senator Tydings, reviewing the doubling of the number of federal judges, says, "The statistics disparage the suggestion that more judges alone are an answer to the problem."[10] Judge John S. Hastings, Chief Judge for the Seventh Circuit, says, "We shall never solve the pressing problems relating to delay and congestion in the Federal Courts merely by appointing additional judges."[11] Judge Albert V. Bryan, Fourth Circuit Court of Appeals, adds that the remedy is not more judges but "better housekeeping within the judiciary itself."[12] I am deeply concerned that these thoughts not be taken out of context. At times additional judgeships are imperative. This was so, for example, at the time of these lectures, for some New York State courts, although the New York courts were subsequently expanded. The point is rather that more judges are not enough; other remedies in addition are imperative.

No one has developed clearly the reason that the increase in number has been so unsuccessful. Inevitably, the upping of the number increases administration—judges' committees are formed, meetings are held, time is lost in moving cases to this judge, deferring the earlier order of that judge, and so on; but we have no statistical estimate of how substantial the delay is. Judge Hastings has said that the more judges, "the more inefficiency creeps into the whole system."[13] It may be that matters have become more complex in the course of the decade; the trend toward complexity and some suggestions as to what to do about it is the topic of Chapter III. Finally, although the judicial recruitment system has been capably and conscientiously administered, it may be that either the pay or the attractiveness of the job has been too small to bring to the bench the quality that is needed. On the state side, this is unquestionably true.

But for whatever reason, we are dealing with a disastrous situation. Before I recite the usual statistics, let me continue to relate the matter in personal terms.

At any given moment, my office in Phoenix, Arizona, has from 1500 to 2000 court matters of every type pending, ranging from an uncontested adoption to civil litigation involving very large sums, and including criminal cases from traffic violations to antitrust suits and murder. I personally in the year 1967, apart from all other work, was in about three dozen cases deeply enough to feel a sense of personal involvement and to have first-hand knowledge of their courses. These were principally in my own state, but they also included substantial matters in other states and ranged through the state and federal systems from courts of original jurisdiction through intermediate appellate courts to the State and Federal Supreme Courts. Before reciting my sorry figures, let me ask one word of personal indulgence. Temperamentally, I tend to be of the "let's-get-on-with-it" type. In some of these cases, it was not to the client's interest to hustle the matter, and I did not; but in most of them, the figures reflect what results when counsel does his best.

Out of more than thirty matters, the number which came speedily to final disposition was six. Most of these were suits relating to the award of public contracts, and in each case, because the construction work could not go forward without determination of the award, the courts were inclined to give a priority. One was a divorce case with an agreed property settlement and hence a default, which took only a few months. Several of these cases moved, quite literally, in days or weeks. One case, in Wisconsin, involved the legality of a contract for a major civic development in which the overall construction cost could run to $10,000,000. Here the litigation ran about nine months from complaint to judgment, with eleven days in court in between.

At this point, the speedy life terminates. On matters still pending, a federal antitrust criminal matter appears to be heading for at least a four-year life, an Indian tax matter in California was two years getting to trial and has a full life of at least four, and a still-pending auto accident controversy involving a default has at least a four-year minimum life, including appeal. A public land matter in Nevada has a more than five-year probable life. Litigation of an important public nature, a group of three matters relating to conflict of interest laws, was in the state trial court, the state supreme court, and had a momentary and breathtaking possibility of a further life in the United States Supreme Court; alas, two votes were not enough to get review. Five years. A piece of trial court commercial litigation was four and one-half years from complaint to judgment. Another contract case involving about $250,000 got its trial court judgment in 1967, after five years; a petty $7,000 matter took a similar time, but got through an appeal. An administrative appeal in California has been moving for two and one-half years.

Let me mention the time champs. A few years ago I completed a litigation program on one matter involving several cases and two receiverships, and it took seven years altogether. In the year 1968, I hope to wind up what is possibly the biggest time botch in the federal system, a seven-year commercial litigation on one case, which has been tied up in two judicial deaths, delayed for several new appointments, had proceedings before three visiting federal judges, and is now happily ensconced in the bosom of the Court of Appeals.* But this defers in seniority to a nine-year shareholders' suit in which I was (unsuccessfully) engaged this year on a final petition for certiorari.

The median time on these cases is between three and four years. If I may attempt what is clearly a subjective judgment as to fair time for these particular matters in a well-ordered legal system, with an effort to make completely realistic judgments and not to ask for greater speed than common sense permits, they represent an aggregate of approximately fifty years of unreasonably and undesirably lost time. In human and personal economic terms, the story is one of frustration, bitterness, and loss. Some of this group are criminal cases, and I put them aside; clearly they should move more quickly than they do and this is so obvious that it becomes a truism to tell this story. But on the civil side, engaging in a lawsuit of any magnitude may be equated to taking a pig into the parlor; the litigant will be mighty tired of the odor before he gets rid of it.[14]

Two of these cases are Indian cases which go to the vitals

---

* As I edit these notes later in 1968, I must report that this case has at least two years more of life expectancy.

of decent existence for the people involved. Two of the cases, in which the same ultimate client is basically involved, involve financial issues which go to the very survival of one of the major economic enterprises of our state; although these are all now happily resolved, they have been a financial blight as long as they existed. Two of the cases mean some hundreds of thousands of dollars apiece to commercial enterprises that have been unable for years to make effective or sensible plans concerning these assets. One involves the availability of a particular kind of health insurance for a large slice of the country's population and one involves the problem of whether some family is ever going to get paid as a result of an auto accident. In one relatively minor matter, all that is involved is approximately $20,000 and, happily, each side can stand the indecision; but the case was filed in the first half of 1964, was tried after the first half of 1967, and was finally set for retrial at the end of 1967, all without ever having left the trial court. In 1968, the case was finally ready to start all over again, three and one-half years old, already having cost both sides in legal fees more than the difference between the settlement offers the day the case began.

Let me get to the fundamental moral issue involved; a legal system should not treat people like this. A man ought to be able to do business without waiting five years to find out whether he is financially alive or dead. This is 10 per cent of a man's adult life, largely spent in waiting for a court to reach him. The best that can be said for a legal system of ordered relationships that takes this long to come to a result is that the system is simply no good; it fails to perform the job the community should reasonably expect of it.

The situation in my personal practice is not much removed from the general condition of the federal courts around the country. New civil cases are being filed in the federal district courts at the rate of about 71,000 a year. The docket situation is getting worse: there were 74,000 cases pending in 1965, 79,000 in 1966, and about 80,000 in 1967; in other words, the federal courts have fallen 6,000 or so more civil cases behind in the last three statistical years. About 17,000 federal cases have been pending for more than two years, and about 8,000 have been waiting for more than three. From 1941 to 1967, federal civil filings increased 84 per cent (from 38,500 to 71,000), and pending civil cases increased over 170 per cent (from 29,000 to 80,000).[15]

The median waiting time in the federal courts in Brooklyn for cases actually tried is now three years, and 10 per cent of the cases are taking more than four years to be heard. In Manhattan, the situation is far worse; there the median case waits almost four years, and 10 per cent are taking well over five. In Civil Court of the City of New York, as its administrative judge Gittleson has said, "Our situation is fast becoming hopeless." He adds that his ninety-five-judge court has a backlog of 150,000 cases—just trying the backlog would take five or six years; but more than 100,000 cases are added each year.[16] The situation in Philadelphia is about one year worse than Brooklyn. In Cleveland and in Chicago, conditions are somewhat better. There the median wait is about two years, although in both cities 10 per cent of the cases are taking almost four years to be heard.

The federal cases, although important, are only a small patch on the total body of litigation in the United States. Phoenix and Tucson in my own state, with an aggregate population of fewer than a million people, have around 20,000 new cases a year in the state courts, or about a third of the whole federal total. Total national federal civil filings are 71,000 a year, whereas filings of all sorts in the state trial courts in Los Angeles are about 180,000.[17] The relation of the civil flood to its criminal parallel is discussed in Chapter III. As a result, although delays are bad on the federal side, they are likely to be worse on the state side.

Let me put the problem in terms of a routine human experience. In December, 1967, John and Mary Jones drive downtown together to do a little Christmas shopping. John has taken the afternoon off from his position as an associate professor at the local university, where he earns about $12,000. The family car is four years old. John and Mary have the group health insurance program of the university, and, in this respect a little abnormally, they also have collision insurance on their car. At the corner of Vine and Elm, they stop for a red light. As they are stopped, the light itself goes completely out and a moment later, before they can decide what to do, they are rear-ended by a truck whose driver, seeing no light, failed to stop in time. There is something to be said for the driver because the light was out, but on the other hand, he probably should have been able to stop in time to avoid a standing car. Perhaps John, who was driving, should have been a little more alert in getting out of the way when the light went out.

Mary has had some real discomfort, but is out of the hospital by Christmas. John has had a somewhat rougher time, having some injury both to the muscles of his back and neck and to two of the neck vertebrae. He will have some stiffness and discomfort from it. Their health insurance has covered the hospital and doctor bills, and their collision insurance has enabled them to get the car back on the road. But they have a legitimate claim for real damages to themselves. The trucking company will pay nothing, and John and Mary would like that traditional American right, a jury trial, to determine their recovery of damages.

The Christmas in question was in 1967, and they were ready to bring their suit by late summer, 1968. To determine when they can expect results, we look to one of the excellent publications of the Institute of Judicial Administration, which tells us the condition of court calendars in various parts of the country. If John and Mary live in Detroit, their case on their 1967 accident will probably come to trial in early 1971. If they are at the University of Hawaii, they can wait until the middle of 1971. If they live in New York, on the Manhattan side of the East River, they will wait until the end of 1971, whereas if they live in the Bronx or Brooklyn, they can look forward to a trial in the middle of 1972. If the university is Pennsylvania, they will have a date with the judge for early 1973. If the medical report for which their lawyer was waiting comes in so that he files the action on September 1, 1968, in Chicago, and if the other side answers with reasonable promptness, the case of John and Mary against the trucker will be heard just in time for Christmas, 1973; although if the case is in the Chicago Municipal Court, it will come up well into 1974.

This, of course, assumes that conditions get no worse between 1967 and 1974. This would be an overly optimistic prediction. In Chicago between 1966 and 1967, because of good work in the circuit court, time was cut by five months, but it rose seven months in the municipal court at the same time. Philadelphia slid about three and a half months farther behind between 1966 and 1967. Manhattan tobogganed a full ten months farther in arrears in that one year, and lost three months more in the year following. Last year in Los Angeles, lawsuit time got four months worse than the year before. If both John and Mary are sixty at the time of the accident, the chance that the two of them will be alive to attend that trial in 1974 is 79 per cent. Should it turn out that their nice little accident happens to involve a nice little law point, so that the case is appealed by one side or the other, and if there should then have to be a new trial, the course of the matter will take five to ten years in any of these cities; if it lasts ten years, the couple's survival chance is 57 per cent.[18] But, to be hideously callous, John and Mary might as well die so far as this litigation is concerned. A good recovery before fees and costs would only be $6,000 or $7,000.

The worst of the delay is the strain on people. The John and Mary case is deliberately chosen as one in which the world won't come to an end whether they get the money or not; the car and the doctor bills were taken care of by their own insurance. The worst feature of the accident is that the pig has been put in their parlor. If they are the tough-fibered type, they may be able to shove the whole episode to the rear shelf of the mind and forget it; but person after person cannot forget and for them, the matter is a constant source of worry and concern. If John and Mary are the ones sued, and if their insurance is on the thin side, they will spend all those years worrying about the impact of the lawsuit on their retirement plans. All too often, John may fail to recover as rapidly as otherwise he might because of a kind of lawsuit morbidity.

If a savage tormentor were attempting to devise an instrument for mental cruelty, he could scarcely improve on the device of leaving simple human beings in severe doubt, for years on end, as to the practical consequences of the normal affairs of life. Waiting time in 1967 or 1968 was over two and one-half years in San Francisco, and was two or three years in Atlanta, Honolulu, Kansas City, Baltimore, in all the large cities of Massachusetts, in Pontiac, Michigan, in Minneapolis, in several cities in New Jersey, and was far worse than this in most large cities of New York. In twenty-seven counties of more than 750,000 people in 1968, the average time from answer to trial in personal injury cases was over two and one-half years. In urban America, this means most of us. If a fundamental social value of the rule of law is to permit people to settle their disputes in an orderly and efficient way, then the system itself is failing, breaking down, as Senator Joseph Tydings has put it, from the vice of sluggishness.[19] We are brought snub up to the bleak observation of the Chief Justice; perhaps the rule of law in this nation cannot endure.

The gloom is unadulterated by a ray of hope. In 1968, we are at the moment of the exhaustion of reform: the patient is dying and there is no miracle drug. All we can do at the moment is look for a cure.

To understand fully how blank is the wall that confronts us, it is necessary to review briefly the course of reform to the present time. In the nineteenth century, the problems of delay, cost, and inefficiency were acute. The two most obvious evils of that century were the division of courts into two systems of law and equity, and the immense complexity of the pleading of the time.[20] Over great resistance, immense progress was made both in unifying the legal system and in simplifying the pleading. The Field Code, sponsored by David Dudley Field in New York, substantially reformed procedure and administration. By the present time, its principles have been adopted almost everywhere. But for all the progress of the Field Code, by 1900 it was widely apparent that justice took too long, cost too much, and was often perniciously unjust. By common consent, the starting point usually taken for a larger reform movement was Roscoe Pound's 1906 speech to the American Bar Association on "The Causes of Popular Dissatisfaction with the Administration of Justice."[21]

In the Pound address, for the first time in an important way, someone not merely criticized the procedure, but also the legal system, attacking inefficiencies in the selection of judges, the waste inherent in overlapping court jurisdiction, and the waste of judicial manpower through inefficient operation. Pound scored the "sporting theory of justice," a theory that a lawsuit was like a football game, to be settled by surprise and trick plays. To illustrate supertechnicality, he cited Missouri, where 20 per cent of the cases in the appellate courts involved points of appellate procedure. He noted that, "In Volume 87, of fifty-three decisions of the Supreme Court and ninety-seven of the Court of Appeals, twenty-eight are taken up in whole or in part with the mere techniques of obtaining a review. All this is sheer waste, which a modern judicial organization would obviate."[22] He decried the practice of "consuming the time of courts with points of pure practice, when they ought to be investigating substantial controversies." He contrasted the English system, under which a population of 32 million people handled its business with 95 judges, with that of Nebraska, population approximately 1 million, where 129 judges were employed for the same purpose. Although he obscured important differences, Pound made an important point: "These 129 are organized on an antiquated system and their time is frittered away on mere points of legal etiquette."

The Pound speech started a movement. A Section of Judicial Administration was created by the American Bar Association in 1913. Also in 1913, the American Judicature Society was founded.[23] This organization has concentrated on the selection, tenure and pay of judges and other court officers, court organization and administration, judicial statistics, and other matters of judicial administration. Its monthly journal, now more than fifty years old, is the most valuable documentary history of the efforts toward improvement. Its primary goal for many years has been the promotion of the Missouri Plan for the nonpolitical selection of judges, and it has been sponsoring conferences around the country on court improvement. I shall come back to its activities in a moment.

From its founding in 1913 until 1936, the ABA Section of Judicial Administration was active principally in a self-instructional sense; interesting and informative papers were read at annual meetings, but there was little overt action. The active years for this Section began in 1937 when Arthur T. Vanderbilt, later Chief Justice of New Jersey, became President of the American Bar Association, and Judge John J. Parker of the Fourth Circuit became Chairman of the Section. The program that emerged was partly a series of developments from the earlier Pound proposals, and partly a completely independent program; the key goals of the Section in the Vanderbilt-Parker period were the regulation of practice by rules of court rather than by legislation; a unified system of courts; the application of business principles to judicial administration; the elimination of surprise through discovery; the use of pretrial hearings; the enlargement of the discretion of judges; and the simplification of the rules of evidence.

Let me now backtrack for a moment. The activities of the ABA Section and of the American Judicature Society were largely directed toward state matters. Meanwhile, there was a titan on the federal scene. As early as 1908, President William Howard Taft was advocating procedural reforms of the utmost importance. He advocated the creation in the federal system of unified procedure for law, equity, and admiralty, which was not finally achieved until 1966. He pressed for the revisions that led to the Federal Equity Rules of 1912.

But Taft's maximum leadership came later, as Chief Justice of the United States. He obtained the passage of the Certiorari Act in 1925, which has so established the jurisdiction of the United States Supreme Court as to keep it far more current with its docket than most of the other courts of the land. But of more general importance, he was the first high figure in the legal system of the country to see the need to give the Supreme Court "legislative" power in the form of rule-making authority, in order for it to deal with cases by the thousands with a single rule rather than by one-at-a-time decisions. As Chief Justice, he originated the legislation that authorized the modern rule-making process; his protégé, William D. Mitchell, became President Hoover's Attorney General and backed the legislation. Although the necessary legal authorization did not come from Congress until after Taft's death, Mitchell eventually became chairman of the committee from which the original civil rules came.

This legislation permitted the most momentous reforms of the twentieth century. Heroes in retrospect are the then Dean of the Yale Law School, Charles E. Clark, who became reporter for the federal rules committee, and his assistant, Professor James W. Moore of Yale. The superb products of their work, and of the Mitchell committee, and of the Supreme Court, which promulgated the rules, were the Federal Rules of Civil Procedure. Putting aside all major details of those rules, they had two blockbusting effects. First, their nontechnical approach to problems of pleading has radically diminished the amount of time to be spent on how people shall ask for relief or object to it; this great clog in judicial efficiency is gone. Second, the rules made universal the system of discovery, or of the devices for finding out about the other fellow's case before trial. This has two major consequences. First, it goes a long way to meet Pound's 1906 objection to litigation by surprise. No one needs to be surprised any longer, and the number of surprise cases has plummeted. Second, the system if it works well should take many controversies out of the courthouse, off the court dockets, and away from the load on court time. To the extent that under the discovery procedures people can exchange information outside the courtroom, they do not need to exchange it within the courtroom; they need only put it into evidence.[24]

When Taft came to the Supreme Court, the individual district judges were local satraps, controlled only rarely by anyone. Given life tenure, negligible supervision, and even less help, they floundered with the problems of their districts as though they ruled over unrelated principalities. This state of affairs Taft thought all wrong. He conceived of the federal legal system as a unit headed by the Supreme Court. He wanted adequate statistical studies to show how well the individual judges were doing their jobs, methods of moving judges from underworked to overworked districts, and leadership for the system. To achieve that leadership, Taft conceived and carried through the creation of the Judicial Conference as a working division of the court system. As he saw it, the judges themselves could become a control committee, exercising the leadership so clearly needed. In originating this program, Taft began a system which has been brought to its greatest utility under Chief Justice Warren.

Law reform was largely in eclipse during World War II. After the war, the independent efforts of a special committee of the American Bar Association under Judge John Parker were merged with the Section of Judicial Administration.

The principal accomplishments of the years up to 1957 were those of Chief Justice Arthur T. Vanderbilt, who wrote widely on administrative reform, originated the invaluable Institute of Judicial Administration of New York University, and led the way to a complete reorganization of the courts of New Jersey. Without doubt, he was the country's most effective man in one state in this century. Yet for all his valiant effort, in New Jersey counties with a 1960 population of approximately three million persons, the average waiting time for a personal injury case in 1967 was two years, about two months longer than it had been in 1966; it improved a little in 1968.

By 1957, reform in the United States was in the doldrums. The Supreme Court had disestablished its committee on civil procedure, so that no work was being done in the federal system outside of the excellent statistical studies of the administrative office for the federal courts and the individual efforts of Chief Justice Warren. The Section of Judicial Administration of the ABA had hit rock bottom: it had nineteen committees, many of which had made no reports for the preceding year; indeed, many of the chairmen did not know what they were supposed to be doing. Membership then had sunk to five hundred; today it has risen to six thousand.

The difference was Justice Tom Clark of the Supreme Court, around whom has swirled virtually every effort to improve the legal services of the states from 1957 to date. At that time, Clark became Chairman of the Section of Judicial Administration. Noting that the administration of justice was "inefficient, slow, cumbersome, and costly," he set to work at once on a major program. He joined Chief Justice Warren and Judge John Parker in devising a new bill to re-establish the rule-making procedures of the federal courts and then took an active hand in seeing the bill through

Congress. As a result, the rule-making procedures since 1960 have been effective.

The details of the Clark activities are fully covered elsewhere;[25] it is sufficient to note here that they were wondrous and endless. He put his full weight behind the program of the American Judicature Society for the improvement of court structure, judicial selection, and court administration, and long strides toward the achievement of the AJS objectives have been made during this period. But the new instrument largely created under Clark's leadership, and his most important contribution, has been the program of improvement of justice by the education of judges. The National Conference of Trial Judges has been a Clark project that has resulted in excellent educative programs, some of the most valuable of which have been aimed particularly at a reduction of congestion by improved administration in the metropolitan centers. Clark's most valuable single contribution has been the National College of State Trial Judges, which conducts month-long programs in various parts of the country, operating principally from its headquarters in Reno, Nevada. Every report shows that this program has made a major contribution to better and speedier justice.

As of January, 1968, there were twin giants at the head of the law reform activities of the United States. On the federal side, Chief Justice Warren was in driving support of every worthwhile activity.[26] On the state side, Justice Clark was the dominant figure: in the year 1967, he was the Chairman of the Board of the American Judicature Society, the head of the Institute for Judicial Administration, a leader in the American Bar Association, and the head of the National College of State Trial Judges. The former head of the Antitrust Division had become virtually a one-man monopoly of law reform in the states.

What is tragically important in this history is that despite the efforts, the legal system is not getting the job done. The plain fact is that people and their problems multiply faster than court improvements. The Chief Justice speaks of the end of the system. As I said in my review of Justice Clark's decade of work between 1957 and 1967, "To go to the end result, in 1957, judicial procedures were 'inefficient, slow, cumbersome and costly.' In 1967, they are still 'inefficient, slow, cumbersome and costly.' It is not the millennium; the increase in the number of cars turned out by Detroit in a year can make the legal system more impossible than anything the administrators can do about it."[27]

What is even more important is that at this moment we are very nearly out of ideas. Let me demonstrate this with precise technical references, and in some depth.

Professor Maurice Rosenberg of Columbia University is a pre-eminent expert on judicial administration. In 1965 he reviewed all of the major pending proposals for basic improvement.[28] One such proposal is the device of eliminating or minimizing auto accident cases, a proposal to which I shall return; it is major and it may be helpful. A second proposal in which, for a time, there was some confidence was that auto accident cases might be divided in half, with a first trial as to whether the defendant was liable, and, if he was, a second as to the amount of the verdict. If the jury found the defendant not liable, there would be no need to take the evidence on damages. In 1960, this had been held out as an optimistic possibility; by 1965, Rosenberg could demonstrate that it was working out unjustly. It did save time, but it also radically changed the results of the cases; he concluded, "As a cure for delay, it ought to be regarded as too heroic for use, at least until a way is found to test and evaluate its effect upon the outcome of the trial."

A second major proposal has been the pretrial conference, based on the hope that the judge at the conference could cut down on the number of issues to be tried, focus the case on exact matters, and thus reduce trial time. I have myself been an ardent advocate of this device. The foremost state in promoting it had been New Jersey, under the leadership of Chief Justice Vanderbilt. But at the request of the Supreme Court of New Jersey, Professor Rosenberg made a comprehensive study in that state that clearly supports the conclusion he stated in 1965: "Contrary to the beliefs of many eminent judges and lawyers, pretrial conferences, when used routinely in personal injury cases, are not the answer to court delay." New Jersey has now made pretrial optional for many purposes. Judge Charles Hardy, an excellent trial judge in Phoenix, Arizona, who had long been an advocate of an invariable pretrial procedure, has reported to me that he has changed his mind and no longer uses pretrial on most personal injury cases. I give up this ghost with extreme reluctance, and will come back to the matter with affirmative suggestions in Chapter III; but for purposes of the immediate discussion, what is significant is that there is no longer widespread faith in this method.

Another device is compulsory arbitration of small claims; Rosenberg reviews its operation in Pennsylvania, and concludes that it "does not warrant adoption as an antidote for delay in major courts." Massachusetts had expanded with what it called the auditor's system or the device of referring some matters in personal injury cases to auditors to report to the court. Rosenberg reports that this method has "not been effective in reducing burdens," and that therefore there had been an important recommendation to abandon it in Massachusetts. Professor Rosenberg, canvassing the entire field of all of the major proposals or devices for the elimination of court delay in the United States, comes to this sad conclusion which I must adopt as my own:

> Viewed as a whole, the campaign had gone forward with much vigor but with no real breakthrough. There has been a definite pattern to the activity. The sponsors of a new device trumpet it as a miracle remedy, manage to get it introduced and almost instantly pronounce it a lavish success. After a time, experience and careful research deflate the premature boasts and then something new is invented. Today it can be fairly said that there is no acceptable evidence that any remedy so far devised has been efficacious to any substantial extent. Only a few of the new measures have worked even to a modest extent, and some of them have been positively counter-productive on the efficiency scale. More important, many of them have had unsuspected side effects in changing the outcome of appreciable numbers of lawsuits.[29]

Professor Rosenberg is no pessimist, and he is not alone. Professor Charles Alan Wright of the University of Texas is one of the most imaginative and creative specialists in procedure in the United States, author of the current edition of an eleven-volume work in the field, and a member of the top procedural committee of the federal system. In 1966, in response to remarks that the Chief Justice had made, Professor Wright published in the *American Bar Association Journal* certain suggestions for improvements in the legal system.[30] At that time I wrote him, noting that his suggestions, although commendable, were not really substantial enough to make any great difference in the flow of the legal work in the United States. Professor Wright responded in agreement, saying, "The Chief Justice has called for fifty thousand planes and I have given him a dozen Piper Cubs."[31]

More formally, in April, 1967, Professor Wright gave the Sibley Lectures at the University of Georgia. His topic was "Procedural Reform: Its Limitations and Its Future." He says two things that are at the heart of these lectures of my own: "The problems of calendar congestion and delay that lie in the future will not be met, in any significant way, by changes in procedure." And again, the identical point being made here, "Since the adoption of the civil rules there has hardly been a significant new idea in the area of civil procedure."[32]

Let us turn to what is actually happening among the reformers on the national scene. The annual address of the Chief Justice is made to the American Law Institute, the country's foremost working enterprise of judges, professors, and lawyers, assembled to improve the general body of the American law. The Institute now has before it only one important project directly relating to procedure, and this is a plan to revise the jurisdiction of the federal courts. Included in that plan is one suggested radical alteration of the legal system: it is a proposal so to change the rules of jurisdiction as to move each year approximately ten thousand diversity cases, or cases between citizens of different states, out of the federal system and into the state courts. This proposal does warmly commend itself to a majority of my brothers of the American Law Institute, a conclusion to which I must regretfully note my dissent.[33] I see immense benefit to the legal system either from speeding cases or from eliminating entirely some from the legal system. I see no benefit in simply moving them from one court system to another. In 1967, the median time for a case actually tried in the Southern District of New York (Manhattan) was forty-five months on the federal side and, for a personal injury case, in 1968 was forty-three months on the state side. In Brooklyn federal time was thirty-six months and the state time was forty-seven months. There is no apparent profit in moving cases from one log jam to another.

The other principal activity in the federal system is the work undertaken by the various committees of the Judicial Conference to improve the rules of procedure. These committees are immensely conscientious; I have served with the committee on civil procedure for eight years under the chairmanship of Mr. Dean Acheson and, for most of the time, with Reporter Professor Ben Kaplan of the Harvard Law School. The entire work has been under the diligent superintendence of Judge Albert Maris of the Court of Appeals for the Third Circuit, and of Chief Justice Warren himself. Excluding my own role as simply another committee member, I have no doubt at all but that the job could not be better or more conscientiously done than under this leadership. With all respect even for the late Charles Clark, I doubt if there has ever been a reporter to equal Professor Kaplan for the combination of thoroughness, reliability, and imaginativeness.

We may therefore conclude that this branch of the work of law reform is moving forward as well as it can move at this moment; and it is this conclusion that gives poignancy to the observation of Professor Wright that nothing in the prospects for changes in procedure will materially affect calendar congestion or delay. We are, I believe, improving justice by the procedural work; and we are improving efficiency in relatively minor ways; but we are not and probably cannot on the basis of any existing proposals reach the heart of the problem. We have dealt with such matters as how to substitute parties when someone dies or when a public official is replaced; we have dealt with how to know when a lawsuit is over, or when appeal time should begin to run;

we have considered which parties need to be included in a lawsuit, and how to determine this question; and, roughly simultaneously with these chapters, we shall submit to the bar of the country a series of suggestions for altering the practices of discovery. If our suggestions are good, and for the most part I think they are, we will save some court time and we will save some money. I know that we have done our best. But again, the full adoption and operation of all of these proposals will probably not bring enough improvement in the legal system to make up for the drag that will be caused by the expansion of the American population from 200 million to, say, 210 million.

The Arden House conference of 1965 should serve as a final demonstration that we have hit a blank wall. This was a superbly conscientious effort by the American Assembly to explore what it termed the "crisis in judicial administration." What is so heartbreaking about the result is that probably a better group could not have been gathered, nor a better try made. It included businessmen, university officers and professors, judges, lawyers, and a thorough cross-section of everyone in the United States who has been worried about judicial administration. The principal working document was a carefully collected group of papers, edited by Professor Harry W. Jones of Columbia University.[34]

The conferees made eighteen recommendations. They might well all be adopted; but like our work in the field of civil procedure, they would more improve the quality of justice than materially affect its timing. Ten of the proposals concern court administration, and the selection, tenure, education, and compensation of judges. All would help; none, I suspect, would help much. Five more of the proposals principally concern criminal law matters; only one is much directed to volume, and that relates primarily to the important but separable matter of minor offenses. I shall come back to the subject, but no solution of these problems would greatly affect the general flow of civil litigation. Two other conclusions of the conference were a general but somewhat qualified approval of trial by jury and an endorsement for each state of citizens' committees on the courts.

The two recommendations directly focused on court congestion problems are principally related to automobile accident cases. The tentative nature of these suggestions confirms that the country is at the moment unsure of any long steps. The American Assembly concluded that "New measures must be devised" to deal with auto accidents, and called for the exploration of various suggestions. The remaining suggestions simply concern the transfer of judges to points where needed, obviously desirable and useful, and the full and effective use of court buildings at all seasons of the year.

That's where we are. Our leading professor from Columbia tells us, accurately, that none of the ideas which looked good at the beginning of the 1960's had proved itself by the second half of the decade. Our professor from Texas tells us that there is no real salvation by changes of civil procedure, and that there have been no truly significant developments in that area, from the congestion standpoint, since the 1930's. As one actively engaged in the contemporary efforts for improvement, I confirm this. Approximately seventy public-spirited Americans met at Arden House, well prepared, thoughtful, and earnest; and the only really significant suggestion they could offer was that we explore proposals to find a wholly different system for dealing with auto accidents.

Against this background of frustration and defeat, I come to the main theme of these chapters:

We must break the shackles on justice. We must meet the challenge of Chief Justice Warren. The rule of law in this nation must endure. What we took from George Washington and John Marshall, what was preserved on this continent by Abraham Lincoln, what we cherish as the great contribution of the English-speaking people cannot be allowed to bloat into immobility. We must find a way.

II

A New Agenda

From the beginning of this century until about 1960 we had at least had an agenda for discussion, a list for action. That agenda was well articulated by Pound and carried forward by Vanderbilt and Parker and Taft and Charles Clark and Tom Clark, and by Chief Justice Warren. What we need for the last third of this century is a new agenda.

This project simply cannot be allowed to be beyond our national talents and beyond our national resources. I take for my analogy that dreary moment after World War II when victory in the field was being followed by disaster in the homes of Europe. At that moment, a great Secretary of State, George Marshall, directed his senior adviser, George Kennan, to gather together the ablest advisers in the country and to prepare for the Secretary the recommendations for the reconstruction and rehabilitation of Europe. The Secretary gave his adviser only one direct instruction. It was, "Avoid trivia."[1] What resulted was the Marshall Plan, and the reconstruction and rehabilitation of Europe.

We need a Marshall Plan for the reconstruction and rehabilitation of the legal system of America. Here, too, as Secretary Marshall said, "The patient is sinking while the doctors deliberate."[2] Like the Marshall Plan, we must have a radical plan for law reform; as Dean Charles Joiner of

Wayne University Law School has accurately said, "Few lawyers wish to be so characterized, yet procedure reform and honest appraisal demand radicals."[3] This radicalism is particularly desirable in procedural reform, where every improvement requires a balance of the plus factors of the improvement as against the negative inconvenience of the change. Improvements therefore ought to be substantial; otherwise they are merely tinkering aggravations.

Once again, Chief Justice Warren is leading the way, with the effective support of Judge John Hastings, senior judge of the Seventh Circuit and Chairman of the appropriate Committee of the Judicial Conference. He backed the bill for the creation of a legal center to stimulate, coordinate, and conduct research studies in all areas of federal judicial administration and to carry on educational programs for judges. At his instance, on February 6, 1967, President Johnson in a message to Congress said, "The mere addition of judges to the courts will not bring about the efficient administration of justice that simple justice demands."[4] He recommended the Federal Judicial Center, the need for which has been described by Warren Olney III, the Director of the Administrative Office of the United States Courts, in testimony before a Senate Committee thus:

> There has been and is no organization for studying the problems of the courts, for developing accurate and complete information on each of the many factors that make up an administrative difficulty, or for assisting in devising and testing suggested improvements. Out of a total of 6,299 persons in the federal judicial branch, there is not one who is devoting full time to studying and planning how to meet the vast changes that our country and its judiciary are living through.[5]

The bill passed Congress in December, 1967, and the Chief Justice took instant steps to get its program moving: he induced Justice Tom Clark, upon his retirement, to become Director of the new Center, and the Chief Justice is expected to join the Center himself upon his retirement.

May I say parenthetically that the only thing wrong with the plan is that the sum originally proposed to be expended for research is not nearly adequate for the purpose. The 1969 suggestion is $140,000 for research studies, and one would hope that far more than this could be usefully expended, and fast.[6] This is less for research on the entire judicial system than would be spent for research on improving the trigger of a new hand gun for the army. The entire budget for the legal system of the United States, federal, state, and local, including police and law enforcement operations, is some four to five billion dollars, and only about eight tenths of a billion of it is for court expenditures;[7] the total is less than one tenth of the national defense budget. We die in part of creeping penury.

I have been speaking of the exhaustion of legal reform in America, of the impasse of today. As we begin to formulate the agenda for research and discussion, we must start from the premise that tinkering and patching the system will not serve the ultimate need: we have tried every tinker and every patch anyone can think of, and although ofttimes improvements are the result, they are not of the necessary far-reaching dimension. This does not mean that we should stop thinking about small improvements, or promoting them; the work of the American Judicature Society, for example, is to be warmly applauded. But it also means that if we are to have a new agenda for discussion in the balance of this century, we must develop far more radical ideas than we have been exploring of late. We need to reconsider our legal system from the ground up. We need to develop plans

1. To reconstruct the institutions of the law.
2. To reconstruct the job we expect the law to do.
3. To reconstruct the way we do that job.

In the remainder of these chapters, I shall discuss some concrete suggestions for this reconstruction, with a mix of some drastic and some modest suggestions.

Let me begin the task of reconstruction with some observations on the lawyers, who were the students, and who become the judges. The first step in the improvement of justice may well be to improve us. It will be remembered that I have been giving delay figures in terms of a median time, but that I have also given some figures for the most delayed 10 per cent of the cases. In the Southern District of New York, for example, in 1967 the median time was forty-five months, but 10 per cent of the cases were taking sixty-four months. My personal median was three to four years, but I had two seven-year and one nine-year exceptions.

A good share of the problem of the abnormal delay is the dilatory lawyer. As Professor Rosenberg puts it, "Even in a court which dispatches its business promptly, vintage cases are often uncorked at trial."[8] He reports that in a small sampling of cases chosen at random in Pittsburgh, lawyer tardiness was responsible for an extra year of delay in half the cases. Partly the delays are caused by continuances, which for obvious reasons a defendant will almost never refuse a plaintiff, and which a plaintiff may not refuse a defendant because of the comradeship of the Bar. This comradeship is immensely meaningful; I acknowledge that I have probably not refused another lawyer a request for an extension three times in the course of my own practice and that, except where the failure was jurisdictional, I have substantially never taken advantage of another lawyer's failure to be timely.

Some lawyer delay is outright pathological, and the infirmity is frequent enough to clog the records of committees receiving disbarment demands. There is the occasional lawyer who simply cannot get at it; who may wait a year or forever to do simple things such as the routine filing of a complaint, or the entry of a judgment that could easily be done in a few minutes. I have seen rare cases of so complete a breakdown of function that the lawyer falsely reports to the client that he has done things which in fact he has never begun.[9]

Sometimes the extremes of delay may involve not the whole bar but some subculture, as the bar of a particular community or specialization. One of the extremest efforts to break a log jam with an ox prod was the 1967 drive of the federal district court in Philadelphia to catch up the maritime litigation, largely injured persons. Pending cases had risen from three thousand in 1961 to five thousand in 1966. Striking results were obtained by a cleanup drive headed by Chief Judge Thomas Clary. The details of the accomplishment make interesting reading, but I shall note only two quotations here. At a singularly bare-knuckled meeting of the court and the maritime bar, Judge Clary reports:

> We had a particularized situation wherein our main roadblock was the maritime bar. In singling out that bar when we first met with them, we informed them that we were perfectly willing to issue rules or regulations limited to them alone, since from our studies of the available statistics, they alone were at fault. . . .

The slightly gentler Judge Leon Higginbotham then, after quoting the poem

> I live in a sea of words
> Where the nouns and the adjectives flow,
> Where the verbs speak of action which never takes place
> And sentences come and go,

concluded with the following remarks:

> This court and the maritime bar must live and perform in a context which is more than a mere sea of words or platitudes. We want action, demonstrable action, and results, and we urge your support for its absolute accomplishment.[10]

But short of the pathologically incapable, those who do not really function at all, it is the do-it-tomorrow crowd that makes up a mighty horde. The whole structure of the profession lends to dilatoriness, and the more so when dockets are so congested that nothing is ever going to happen anyway. Sometimes the dilatoriness may be for some legitimate tactical advantage; this, I think, is relatively rare. Sometimes it is the product of bad organization of the lawyer's work: he may have too much to do, and the matter may get lost. It has often been suggested that delay may be the product of the desire to pick up another court day or another couple of hours charged. But the shabbier aspects of delay I put aside in order to focus on what has, within my own observation, been the prime cause, a cause so simple as to sound almost silly when said aloud: lawyers and judges are frequently dilatory in their work, and thus delay litigation longer than it needs to be delayed, because in many cases that's the kind of people we are.

The question then arises as to whether anything can be done to change us as people. Here the place to start is in the schools. Indeed, it may be before the student ever gets to the schools, though I hasten to say that I think not. Specifically, many law schools now have more applicants, and frequently many more applicants, than they can accept. This means that choice must be made among applicants on the basis of some kinds of standards. If the school is in the luxurious position of having, say, 600 applicants for 150 seats in the freshman class, then probably the top 50 applicants are fairly obvious and clearly should be admitted. Equally probably, of the next 200, it would make very little difference which 100 were chosen.

The question then arises as to whether this second 200 can be sifted by any psychological tests to sort out the get-things-done-now type from the leave-it-until-tomorrow boys. I have been sufficiently curious about this to examine the matter fairly closely and am satisfied that there are no psychological testing devices in existence that are worth serious consideration for this purpose.[11] In any case, my own spirit shrinks from applying any further mechanical criteria to the selection of law students.

Such a selection process would be in vain in any case because the students are indoctrinated in delay from the moment they hit the law school. A prime lesson learned by many students from three years of law school is that nothing has to be done on time except the final examination, and not always that. It may be that this languorous approach could not be altered without the sacrifice of values perhaps more important than training in expedition, but at least the whole weight of the program is to put a zero premium on timeliness.

Most schools pride themselves on the fact that the student

need not come to class if he doesn't want to; he can come tomorrow. Most teachers do not police recitations or preparedness, so that the student need not be prepared today if he does not want to be; he can be prepared tomorrow if he is ready tomorrow. Some of the great courses in the history of the American law schools have been the case-of-the-month club type, the student caressing with exquisite care every last nuance of a case until exhaustion sets in. The schools require almost nothing to be done in a timely way; the overwhelming bulk of the education to the point of 90 or more per cent is in large classes, with casebooks in which the professor has no fixed design from day to day, but rather intends to go as far as he can get. Assignments of papers and briefs are rare and extensions easy to get. Most schools publish law reviews, put out by the students. Legendarily, most of them come out at any old time; if most of them actually reached the subscribers in the publication month designated on their covers, it would be an incredible accident.[12]

Thus, a reasonably bright boy in a typical law school who registers in September (unless he should be a little delayed) has no performance of any kind expected of him at any time until the following February, and usually the importance of time or timeliness is outright denied in the design and conduct of every course he takes. The antitime element of the training is intensified by the subject matter and the method. Most students are reading cases. Whatever may be said in favor of the case system in terms of its analytical values, it is unquestionably the slowest method of acquiring information that the mind of man can devise. I appreciate that there are blessings of the case method apart from simply finding out what was decided and, within narrow limits, I admire and respect its rigors. The fact remains that it is a method calculated to give its participants the slows rather than the quicks in their approach to the profession. Moreover, when the method is used at its worst, it is far, far slower than it has to be for any achievement of the values attributed to it. Whether the object is to get information, or to analyze, or to "think like a lawyer," the state-the-case method is the most sluggish conceivable device for getting these results. Having a boy rise in place to mumble through some aged summary of a case is not merely wholly antiintellectual, it puts a premium on a leaden-footed approach to the handling of legal business. The great teachers, of course, do not do this, but, alas, not all teachers are great.

To this must be added the other nonaction force of some legal education, the business of teaching by browbeating or outsmarting the student. Let me quote what I said on this subject in *Marble Palace:*

> Contemporaneously, much of the blame rests on legal education. A lad goes to law school to sit before a professor who, if not brighter than he, is at least far better informed on the subject at hand. The method of instruction usually involves an exercise in which the professor leads the student into error and out again, quizzing him to explore what he has learned of his day's lesson. Whatever the student answers will speedily be shown by the professor to be wrong. This device is clean intellectual fun but embarrassing to the student, who quickly learns that a decisive answer will get him into more trouble than one which contains many "if" and "but" escape clauses. The habit of thinking and writing in terms of multiple qualifications is ingrained with final examinations. The student studies the writings of judges who in turn were educated by studying writings of judges.[13]

This has a consequence in terms of writing, but it also has a consequence in terms of incisiveness. It is part of the total force which keeps the student from doing it now.

Parkinson's Law is that "work expands to fill the time available." Since by virtue of the legal system, time is almost always available, our work does tend to fill and overflow the available time; we are a foremost illustration of Parkinsonism. An article by Aronson & Gerard in the *Journal of Personality and Social Psychology* develops a relevant correlary to Parkinson's Law. They present the intriguing principle that if a person has excess time in which to perform a task initially, he will tend to require excess time thereafter; in other words, there is an effect of early excess time on subsequent performance. They say that "those who are allowed excess time to complete a task on the first occasion will spend more time completing a subsequent similar task than individuals who had been allowed a minimum of time on the first occasion."[14] The tests run on groups given varying amounts of time to do the same thing do strongly indicate that those given too much time at the beginning tend to take too much time later.

I do not mean to draw a consequence for legal education from one article, no matter how ingenious; I do draw the consequence from observation. If the law schools are to assist in the problems of judicial administration, one method may be to discourage delay at the beginning. If this is to be done, there must be some emphasis on re-enforcing (rewarding) good behavior (promptness) and extinguishing or punishing bad behavior (procrastination). This requires more emphasis upon the conditions of teaching than upon the characteristics of the learner. At this point, psychologists might well make a contribution to legal education, because the principles of re-enforcement, extinction, punishment, discrimination, generalization, countercondition, shaping, stimulus control, and related concepts are all fairly well established from both animal and human work. The major notions are that human behavior is controlled, in large part, by its consequences, and these consequences can be manipulated in the learning process. If prompt behavior is desired from lawyers, they must "like" to be prompt and "want" to be prompt, and this motivation can be obtained by providing appropriate re-enforcement contingent on promptness. Indeed, I am assured by my psychologist friends that the provision of such re-enforcement in the classroom is relatively easy. Given a few teachers of law who may wish to try out some new ways of teaching that may be beneficial in their own right but that may also allow for specific shaping of promptness behavior, and given a few judges who wish to encourage promptness by means other than punishment to procrastinating attorneys, a worthwhile program of research could be developed.

I therefore put down as item number one on my agenda for the future this *Recommendation:*

> 1. Let us determine whether legal education can be so altered as to reduce dilatoriness in lawyers, and if so, how. If this can be done, does it conflict unduly with other values of legal education, and if so, can this conflict of values be adjusted?

Let me turn to other and very different aspects of legal education. In the Sibley Lecture earlier mentioned, Professor Wright quotes Charles Clark as saying in 1963 that "problems of legal procedure and law administration"[15] have become major subjects for the schools, the bar associations, and the courts. Courts, yes; bar associations, yes; but although it may be impossibly brash to challenge two such experts at once, so far as law administration and the schools are concerned, the statement is unduly optimistic. The collapse of our court system by its very nature is a kind of paralysis that creeps a little more every year, like arthritis slowly climbing the spine. As a result, judicial administration presents what for the schools is a low visibility issue. New York University, Columbia, and the University of Chicago give major attention to law administration; I am not sure that anyone else does. The slightest word of the Chief Justice in an opinion may be subject to comprehensive discussion in the classroom and in the law review; but his concern that there may be a total failure of the legal system of the United States goes largely unnoticed in the schools.

Specifically, the last teachers' directory shows eighteen law teachers, in somewhat fewer schools than this, who are teaching courses in judicial administration. The University of Texas, for example, has had a course regularly for twenty years. Moreover, individual faculty members are deeply involved in reform movements outside the law schools. Again, Texas is an example of a school in which four faculty members are involved in various programs. In Indiana, a Judicial Study Commission draws heavily on the state law schools, and the various statewide Judicial Reform Conferences have professors involved.

I cannot account for the school programs being so modest. Certainly the schools, and the best men in them all over the country, are vibrantly alive to the problems of life as it is lived. There is no retreat to the ivory tower in criminal administration, or in antitrust law, or in labor relations, or in taxation, or in other fields too numerous to mention. But judicial administration has simply not come sharply into focus; as has been well said, "It is a political issue of obviously low intensity."[16] This is not because there has been no direct urging. Chief Justice Vanderbilt in an essay, "The Future of Legal Education," urged that lawyers should be trained to improve the courts of law,[17] and so has Justice Clark. But the idea does not catch fire. This lack of concern is illustrated in depth in the commentary and 1966 report of the Curriculum Committee of the Association of American Law Schools.[18] Full-scale statements by three professors are followed by commentaries by three others, and reports by two more. These are good and useful essays throughout, by good and useful people, including some of the first-rank educators of the country. Professor Eugene F. Mooney of Kentucky rejects "the whole underlying concept" of contemporary legal education because he wishes to build the curriculum around "social values"; and yet he says nothing at all on the social value of making the system work. His interest is in affording legal services to the poor, using social science data and skills, and keeping ahead of the flow of written law; but Professor Mooney does not direct himself to keeping ahead of the flow of cases. An excellent analysis by Professor Abraham S. Goldstein on "Education Planning at Yale" plans education for many things, but not for preventing the collapse of the whole system. Associate Dean Charles D. Kelso of the University of Miami addresses himself to the great needs of the future and calls for specific research projects on criminal law enforcement, land use control, water resource development—everything but judicial administration.

The gap becomes most interesting in the overall report of the Committee, entitled "Models for Curricular Reform," presented by the very able Professor Quintin Johnstone of Yale. The report covers four types of schools, a policy directed school, a legal doctrine directed school, a skills directed school, and a combined purposes law school, but nowhere is there any allusion to the fact that the legal system is not working very well. The complete blackout is most dramatically illustrated in a classification of twenty-two areas of study from which the program of the second and third years should be built for the all-purpose law school.[19] The courses include business organization and administration, manufacturing and distribution, transportation, agriculture, natural resources, labor relations, professions, government organization and administration, leisure activities, the arts, religion, health, deviant and antisocial behavior, and other areas. Not one of these appears on its face to have anything to do with that condition that is the prime responsibility of lawyers and that the Chief Justice of the United States tells us is undermining the whole constitutional system of government. The same gap appears in an unusual and very good four-page *Newsweek* story on new developments in legal education; there is much on the increasing attention to urban and criminal problems, a social shift in the analysis of property problems, an increase in attention to psychiatry and individual research and writing; and, except for one sentence from Professor Geoffrey Hazard, not one word on improving the way the system works.[20]

I submit that this is wrong, and so offer a second *Recommendation* for the agenda:

> 2. Law schools generally should develop for all students comprehensive and meaningful programs on judicial administration.

Recommendation 2 is offered only as a stopgap; it is not a radical suggestion and does not come close to satisfying me. If Professor Johnstone's program had, for example, substituted two credits on the collapsing court system for two credits on leisure activities, the schools would by no means be making the contribution that might be expected of them. The larger question is whether there should be some total reorganization of the curriculum and of the whole method of teaching directed at increasing the effectiveness of the legal system in serving its primary demand. I have spoken of the problem of training in diligence and expedition. Let me turn now to questions not merely of pace, but of a total greater efficiency at whatever speed.

Let me begin with the negative: I do not wish in any material way to increase training in pure craftsmanship at the expense of thought and theory and research. The proliferation of tax courses, for example, seems to me a step in the wrong direction, and, but for the omission to which I have dissented, I like Professor Johnstone's program. But the question remains whether we can improve the effectiveness of the whole legal system by major alterations in both subject matter and method of teaching.

Basically, I would terminate the general use of the case system at the end of the first year and move thereafter to small group projects with much individual attention. This takes more money, more space, more books, and more faculty. This is not the place to weep over the undernourished state of legal education; I can remember the pang I felt when a university president in my own state advocated a new law school to the state legislature on the ground that he could operate one for only half the cost of the English department. Happily, he raised his sights before he got his school.

But assuming that we have the funds and the talent at our disposal, how shall we use it? I continue to be tempted by Jerome Frank's 1933 proposal for clinical law schools in which students would mix some doing with some learning. This does not conflict in my mind with the avoidance of excessive craftsmanship. A much-to-be-applauded example is the current work in Chicago, San Diego, and elsewhere, in which the students become actively involved in Public Defender functions. The work of students in the New York Bail Project was surely worthwhile. There is merit in Chief Justice Vanderbilt's observation that "it is unethical for the young lawyer to practice at the expense of his client."[21] I can recall an episode in which, by some superb mismanagement on our part, a young man in our office saw the first jury of his lifetime when called upon to empanel one in open court. If the working problems can be well enough selected, which means that Bar cooperation is high and faculty time financed to permit superintendence, the student could integrate much of the separately compartmented knowledge offered in the best of schools. A University of California student who apprenticed in our office and there worked on a public lands case that went to the United States Supreme Court, took that very case back to the Berkeley campus for moot court purposes before it was decided in Washington. I visited his "class" and believe that exceptionally effective results were obtained for the students by the reality of the problem.

Certainly if the courts are to function better because young lawyers make them function better, there should be an upswing of emphasis on the courtroom branch of the practice. This means particularly procedure, evidence, trial practice, and appeals. Those courses generally need to be entirely done over. The modern widespread administration of moot court programs I would condemn absolutely as one of the great lost opportunities in contemporary education. The briefing and argument of an appellate case is as exacting, difficult, and important a function as a lawyer can perform. It is equaled in difficulty only by the materially different problems of the trial of the case. Yet in the widespread contemporary law school practice, these functions are frequently taught by students who know absolutely nothing about them to other students who learn absolutely nothing about them. The program normally culminates in a pretentious perform-ance before a distinguished bench, the best the particular community can afford, which sees and hears untutored stu-dents do as well as they can. I am reminded of the biting comment of Professor Geoffrey Hazard on law reviews: "In respect to student work, the wonder is that we should expect anything but recurrent mediocrity from inexperienced re-searchers who are chiefly preoccupied with learning the basic corpus of the law."[22]

This condition is a by-product of the financial shortages of the law schools, for if moot court is to be taught properly, it must be taught with great individuality. Every student's brief ought to be worked over by someone who knows briefs, and to the extent necessary, it ought to be redone and then gone over again. Every argument should be heard and criti-cized by someone highly experienced and competent to make the criticisms. Preferably the arguments should be recorded, and played back for subsequent criticism. I have tried experi-ments of this sort with moot court, and I am aware that Professors Fleming James and Addison Mueller at Yale have given similar intimate attention to other types of basic legal combat. Harvard is proud of its Ames Competition in moot court, and of its third-year trial practice program, guided by able practitioners on and off the faculty. But generally speak-ing, the student gets the best training his school can afford in the law of agency, much of which he could literally teach to himself; and he gets no help at all where he so badly needs it, in the actual arts of advocacy.

Pleading, procedure and evidence have often been in low repute in the schools, and deservedly so if tediously and unimaginatively taught. But excellent works are now available, and poor instruction is not now necessary, if ever it was. An illustration of highly professional training coupled with intellectual discussion is the American Trial Lawyers Association Student Advocacy Program. The program was launched in cooperation with the University of Michigan Law School, where twenty-four films were produced, representative of all the steps in a small personal injury case. Mr. Robert Begam of Phoenix, for the American Trial Lawyers Association, and Dean Charles Joiner, then at the University of Michigan Law School, were particularly involved. For example, there are films dealing with the taking of depositions, the handling of a pretrial conference, jury examination, and so on. Films occupied the first ten or twelve minutes of the class hour, with discussion following. A similar series on criminal matters has since been produced in cooperation with the United States Department of Justice. The Association also runs a popular day-long student advocacy seminar at the law schools.

Legal education should not be longer; a fourth year of the same thing would be an outrage. But it should be much fuller, again a matter of more money to provide more faculty attention to the students. For the bright student, particularly if he is not on the law review, a legal education is not really very demanding; he has abundant time left over, at least once he learns to concentrate on his work. A 1967 poll at the Harvard Law School showed over a third of the third-year law students studying fifteen hours a week or fewer, with almost two thirds under twenty-five hours.[23] I can recall a law student, by no means the brightest in his class, who attended a good law school, worked on its law review, took a master's degree in history at the same time, and had a few music courses to keep busy. I recently visited with a high-stand Columbia law student who is getting a graduate business degree, working in a store for fifteen hours a week, and commuting about fifty miles a day. A good medical school manages to consume its students altogether.

Some suggestion may occur from consideration of the teaching methods of the Frank Lloyd Wright School of Architecture, operating in Arizona and Wisconsin under the direction of the widow and the son-in-law of the great architect. In accordance with the principles of the master, and as he ran the school in his own lifetime, the training concentrates on the study of organic architecture, and the student is expected for the period of his studies to give his whole life to what he is doing, and to reach every aspect of related chore and art there may be. He may work at drafting for a part of the day, help build a needed road on the grounds during another part, and help construct a new wing to a building the day after. By help construct, I mean literally work with the tools. If there is a dance or music program, he is expected to participate to the best of his ability: if costumes are to be made and a stage to be decorated, everyone helps; and the costumes and the stage sets are superb. The program is seven days a week, with a lecture of some sort related to some phase of creative living as part of the Sunday morning breakfast program.

Can legal education borrow something of value from this total approach? Just as the architectural student can profit both from designing a tower and building a road with his hands, so the law student can profit both from a study of the theory of insanity in his criminal law course and from interviewing a prisoner for bail purposes at the jail. Part of the job of the lawyer as a community leader as well as a courtroom advocate is to entertain, whether for its own sake or for a purpose, and systematic theatricals and other entertainments in the law school life could very realistically be part of the training for the total performance. The student may study the operation of the Social Security Act in his law school class; it could mean a great deal more to him if for his law school years he were also a student member of the board of a retirement home. The architects are seeking a planned interaction between the profession and the total business of living; if law schools had a total program, they could do the same thing to the end of greater productivity of their graduates.

The thoughts just expressed are ill-digested and inadequately considered suggestions. This is, after all, an agenda for discussion, not a concrete program for action. But I suggest as a next *Recommendation* for the agenda:

> 3. A reconsideration of legal education to determine whether, without the sacrifice of other important values, it is possible to make the graduates substantially more effective in the handling of cases, both in and out of the courtroom, to the end of increasing the efficiency of the legal system.

We have been speaking of changes in the lawyers, in the students, and in the schools; it remains to speak of changes among the judges.

Here, if it could be done, lies the only total solution to the entire congestion problem. If Superman were to abandon his preoccupation with Lois Lane and the newspaper business to become Superjudge, our entire backlog would evaporate in a hurry. The Superjudges don't have backlogs. When Judge J. Skelly Wright, now of the Court of Appeals of the District of Columbia, was a district judge in Louisiana, he was quite possibly the most effective district judge

in the United States. In the short period since he left the
trial court, it has taken at least four men to handle a roughly
similar docket. The overwhelming bulk of Wright's auto accidents he settled at pretrial, and the remainder he tried at
a rate of about one a day, whereas many a good judge takes
three.

In the State of Oregon there is a federal district judge
named John Kilkenny. With all due deference to the distinguished bench of the Ninth Circuit, so far as I know,
Judge Kilkenny is the most effective single judge in it: when
he has visited our region, the backlog has melted like the
snow. For illustration, he disposed of a $600,000 trial of
some complexity in a day, to the general satisfaction of all
parties. The Oregon district has three judges but, until a
recent appointment, one was protractedly ill. Kilkenny, along
with an exceptionally able colleague, Judge Solomon, has
kept the calendar absolutely current, has regularly the
smallest number of three-year cases in the West, and is able
in addition to travel outside his District to try cases for from
sixty to ninety days a year. Like Judge Wright, he regularly
tries auto accident cases in a day.

In the state court of my own community, there are twenty-
one judges. In the nine-month period ending December 31,
1967, Judge A disposed of 388 cases, Judge B of 385 cases,
Judge C of 367. On the same bench, Judge D disposed of
205 cases, Judge E 280 and Judge F 282. I have chosen the
ambiguous term "disposed of" deliberately—this covers every
way of getting rid of a case. In terms of trials, four judges
heard from 88 to 101 cases, and seven judges heard fewer
than 65 cases. This does not mean that high productivity is
necessarily high quality. One of the high producers, though
he has very great virtues, does tend to be heavy-handed and
arbitrary; one of the low producers is perhaps our ablest

judge, and by no coincidence at all he gets exceptionally difficult cases; and another had much nontrial work in probate. But with all the qualifications of quality, the fact remains that there is a perfectly prodigious range of productivity among judges. If it could be done, the cheapest, easiest, fastest way to cut the backlog would be to bring low-producing judges to a higher level of performance.

A first level of the problem is pay. In my own community, the pay of an experienced trial judge is approximately the same as what a young man about six years out of law school is likely to earn in a large office. The average net income of all law partners in the United States for 1963 was $20,000;[24] The pay of an Arizona trial judge today is $19,500. New York law offices recently raised beginning lawyers' pay to $15,000 a year, whereas the most recent statistics supplied by the Institute of Judicial Administration show the highest judicial salary of the state below $24,000 in more than half the states. The consequence is that it is extremely difficult to get anyone of any quality to take the jobs, and extremely hard to keep good men on the bench after they are there. We had two resignations of able judges in 1967. One, perhaps the most effective judge we have had, left a docket virtually current. He has perfectly forthrightly stated that he left the bench to earn a living. The work is pleasant, but it is not a holy calling, and it has to be paid for. *Recommendation:*

4. Judicial pay and perquisites must be kept at least roughly equivalent to the income of good members of the bar. In some of the states, this will require a radical change.

No one really knows how the best judges are chosen. In

an excellent and comprehensive current collection of readings on the subject, the first article argues for the need to
establish some systematic set of criteria with which to evaluate or rate judges.[25] This very badly needs doing, but to
date neither the law nor the social sciences have given us
an evaluation method, and the consequence is that we have
only highly informed intuitions as to comparative methods
of achieving quality. Every lawyer can compare the state
and federal judges in his own area, but there are so many
differences involved between the jurisdictions that such
comparisons are only a little instructive. Few lawyers, if
any, can make comparisons in depth as to quality among
the judges of different states.

Once we have the evaluations, we can also appraise the
elective judiciary from the standpoint of the time judges
spend going to meetings, meeting people, and raising money
for their campaigns. In this connection we must take into
account the appearance created by the reception of funds
for campaigns, an evil well handled in my own state by a
tradition making contributions extremely small.

Our problem is whether one system is more likely than
another to produce Wrights and Kilkennys. Assuming that
a merit selection system will help quality, a current proposal in California eliminates many of the criticisms of
some merit plans. Under the California plan, sponsored by
the judges under the leadership of Chief Justice Roger J.
Traynor, there were to be a group of recommending bodies
for the state and the various major divisions of it. The
state body would be composed of the Chief Justice as chairman, one judge of a court of record appointed by the Governor, two members of the state bar appointed by it, and
two nonlawyers, appointed by the Governor. The plan
avoids dilution of the Governor's power by giving him a

dominant hand in the selection of the commission, but at
the same time ensures that he will be well informed before
he exercises his power. Chief Justice Traynor, in an address
given simultaneously with these lectures at the dedication
of the Earl Warren Legal Center, noted that Chief Justice
Warren, when he was Governor of California, had begun
the practice of referring state judicial appointments to the
state bar for recommendations. Chief Justice Traynor believes that the California plan "would be one more major
advance in the speedily rising standards of the judiciary in
our state. It would minimize any risk that the executive
power could be used to reward financial or legislative support. It would maximize the possibilities of highly qualified
appointees."[26] *Recommendation:*

> 5. Work should be done to devise a system for the
> measurement of the quality of judges in terms of ef-
> fectiveness and merit. When such tools are devised,
> serious studies should be made of the various methods
> of selection of judges to determine whether in fact
> one method truly is better than another. Meanwhile,
> the California proposal is a worthwhile experiment.

Our trial judges are chosen almost entirely from the prac-
ticing bar. Sometimes they are chosen from a subgroup of
the practitioners, the trial bar, and this is believed to be an
important criterion by the committee of the ABA called
upon to recommend candidates for federal judgeships; but
in many instances, the appointees have no experience in
judging, nor in the business of judicial administration, before they are appointed.

It may be that we should change this system totally and
that our judges should be specially trained in the business

of judging before they become judges at all. In the German system in particular, this is done, and we should consider whether we might profit from the example.[27] Perhaps we might create a system of graduate training for judicial candidates, coupled with programs of office experience in trial offices, plus clerkships with judges. It may be that in jurisdictions where there are two levels of judges, as for example, city or municipal courts and general trial courts, persons could be moved from one to another. It may be, in short, that a person could be trained to be a judge before he becomes one. *Recommendation:*

> 6. We should determine whether the office of trial judge should be a kind of civil service position, to which a person may progress by virtue of special training and examination; we should attempt to develop methods of deciding whether such a system would be as well suited to our needs as the more traditional alternatives.

So long as we are appointing judges wholly untrained in the business of judging, clearly we must educate them after they come to the bench. From thirty to thirty-five new judges are appointed every year in the federal system alone; there were seventy in 1966. Here I have no radical recommendation to suggest even for thought; I can only follow the beginnings that have been made by Justice Clark with the National College of State Trial Judges, in turn based on the educational seminars for federal courts.[28] These are now being followed with Judicial Conferences in the various states and, in New York and California at least, with special programs of more intensive training. Whether the State Judicial Conferences of one or two days are in fact productive enough to be worth the disruption of trial calendars itself warrants critical measurement, for they may on occasion become only extra holidays. But there can be no doubt of the value of the larger programs when well carried out. As the report of the President's Crime Commission relating to courts observes, the careers of judges tend to last up to twenty-five years. Only about half of the newly selected judges have prior substantial courtroom experience and very few have any background in criminal cases. The Commission therefore strongly recommends that there be a real apprenticeship for judges. It "urges expansion of programs for the training of judges, investment of more effort in curriculum development, and experimentation with procedures making participation in continuing programs mandatory."[29]

The value of such programs is dramatized in the experience of a single individual, Judge Irwin Cantor of the Superior Court of Phoenix. Judge Cantor is a conscientious, capable man who was appointed judge with a background principally in commercial law; his courtroom experience was negligible. In his first year, he went to the National College of State Trial Judges. He reports of this experience:

> The first value of the program to me was to give me an overall picture of my new responsibilities. It also gave me answers to specific questions and taught me things I needed to know about administration, particularly in criminal law. Recent Supreme Court decisions on criminal practice were new to me then; I had no clear idea of the type and importance of the records I would be expected to keep on arraignments, for example. One of the most concrete results for me was to make me realize the need to save time for all judges by obtaining uniform jury instructions. I came back sold on this idea and spent two years working on

it with my fellow judges, an effort that was directly triggered by my experience at the College. Now this county does have uniform jury instructions. In that connection it was particularly helpful to learn in detail what the State of Illinois had done in that field and as a result we have followed their example.[30]

Recommendation:

7. The program of the National College of State Trial Judges is a great success, and should be expanded into the federal system. It should be broadened, or duplicated in the states, so as to give all judges an effective opportunity for advanced education both in the substance and the administration of their work; and the exposure to such programs should be recurrent in the course of the judge's career. This should be supplemented by traveling and local education as well.

Let me wind up with a few thoughts on the rebuilding of courthouses. A courtroom does not have to be a box with chairs. The judge does not need to sit behind the witness, unable to see him effectively. For all the oft-spoken piety that the trial judge is in the best position to evaluate the truth of the witness by observing his demeanor, the fact is that by virtue of most courtroom architecture, the judge may have to strain to see. Nor does the witness need to be in profile to the jury, with the jurors twisting to follow what is going on. Nor does there have to be a considerable distance between the lawyers' seats and the witness box. Nor does there have to be an everlasting search for chalk or crayon if an illustration is to be drawn, or an interruption to install movie equipment, or time out to put up a magnetized demonstration board, or a removal of the judge from the bench to the rear of the courtroom so that he can follow what is going on; all of which I have seen. Nor does the courtroom need to be large enough to be an echoing sound-box.

The typical urban courthouse with several courts has no need for more than one or two large courtrooms, if that. The actual litigation areas can be circular or oval so as to avoid strain and improve vision. There can be built-in display equipment, and built-in electrical equipment for everything from the amplification of sound to the display of X rays to the recording of testimony. Offices and chambers can be so arranged that visiting judges can use courtrooms without disturbing a sitting judge tending to business in his chambers, and poor lights and drafts and outside sound disturbances can readily be eliminated: I have personally had to suspend a trial because jackhammers were at work in the street below. Many of these improvements can increase efficiency.

The new courthouse in Marin County, California, is being systematically developed along these lines; it gives special attention to the speediest and most efficient possible use of courthouse and courtroom space.[31] The subject is now receiving active study under the leadership of Judge William S. Fort of Eugene, Oregon, Chairman of the Committee on Courtroom Design and Court Facilities of the Section of Judicial Administration of the American Bar Association.[32] His efforts have resulted in a joint committee with the American Institute of Architects. The two are working jointly with the University of Michigan Law School and the School of Architecture in a project financed by the Ford Foundation, from which changes should come. Meanwhile, the General Services Agency and the Administrative Office of the United States Courts are conducting their own studies of architectural and structural revisions. *Recommendation:*

> 8. Research now under way should be continued and expanded to determine the types of physical facilities most conducive to the speedy dispatch of court business. This will relate to computerized assignment systems, discussed in Chapter IV; but in this connection, consideration should be given to the use of televised assignment systems in large courthouses, after the fashion of flight information in airports.

The first stage of improvement is to share through general recognition what the insiders already know: the administration of the law business of the United States is in a state of disaster right now. It grows worse, menacing the very existence of justice in this country. For all the diligent and creative efforts that have gone into improvement, we have come to the end of the road on existing programs. There is nothing that the profession is seriously ready to accept that will cure the situation. We have lost the last great recourse in which we have put faith, the endless proliferation of judges and courtrooms.

The country is at a low point in its creativity in dealing with this problem. One reason is that almost no serious research is going on in the United States directed to this end. Some kind of breakthrough is imperative. Major research must be enlarged or begun. *Recommendation:*

> 9. The Federal Judicial Center plan as adopted by the Congress, should be activated on a large scale;* and the companion National Court Assistance Act proposed by Senator Tydings should also be adopted.[33]

* Since the date of these lectures, this is beginning to happen.

We must be prepared for radical innovations. We should at least consider altering our program of legal education to reduce the dilatory tendency and increase the effectiveness of the lawyers who handle the courthouse business of our people. We must improve our judicial system by making it more attractive to good men, perhaps by creating an entire program of trained career judges, by determining what are the best methods of selecting judges, and by improving the training of the judges we have. Indeed, it may be necessary to change the very structure of our courthouses, much as one would tackle a log jam in a warehouse by rebuilding the building, in order to increase as well as to perfect the flow of judicial business.

III

*Cutting the Law
Down to Size*

James Kidd was an Arizona copper miner who disappeared in 1949. He left a will with instructions to "sell all my property . . . and have this balance money to go in a research or some scientific proof of a soul of the human body which leaves at death." This will was filed in September, 1965, in Phoenix, Arizona, and the estate proved to be about $225,000.

James Kidd may have been an obscure copper miner when he disappeared, but his will made him famous. The Phoenix bar was deluged with applicants from all over the world. I had to decline one from England because our office had accepted another representation first, and unsuccessfully called seven offices to find a substitute; all were already engaged.

The matter came on for hearing before an exceptionally capable and conscientious trial judge who patiently sat the matter through. There were pretrial proceedings in March and in May, 1967. First predictions were that hearings would last approximately eighteen days, but as the number of claimants grew to approximately 138, hearings continued in the summer of 1967, running on and off over a time period of about thirteen weeks. In September and October, the court time was occupied in part with claims by alleged heirs of Kidd who were attacking the will. The court finally took a week for deliberation and then made a disposition of the fund to an excellent neurological institute in the community for research "in the combined fields of medical science, psychiatry, and psychology."[1]

In so ordering, the court necessarily disappointed the other 137 claimants. These were an intriguing lot. They included, in addition to some well-established organizations explaining psychic phenomena, The Institute of Divine Metaphysical Research, Inc.; The Truth Seeker, Inc.; the Interdenomination Divine Order; the Aquarian Foundation; Soul Search, Inc.; and others. In the course of its deliberations, the court heard a claimant argue that mankind originally was transported to earth two million years ago in flying saucers. This applicant got the information from a "holy being" who directed him to a location in Malabar, California, where he was confronted by a triangular space ship and had a conversation with the person in it. Witnesses claimed all sorts of mystical emanations.

The friend of a departed dentist put on a courtroom demonstration of his continuing powers. Explaining that the soul of her dead friend talked to her by contracting her muscles, she plugged up her ears and placed an electric dryer over her head to convince the court that she could not hear. Her mother stood behind her and asked her simple questions, to which the witness, who could neither see nor hear her mother, nodded or shook her head in reply. Either the dentist or the witness or both batted .666, though they missed whether Barry Goldwater was from Arizona, and whether the day was Saturday. She explained that the departed contacted her through her nervous system to which he was attached "by a cord of light."

The Kidd case is intriguing and, if one is so inclined, amusing; but it also puts a very major question for the business of judicial administration. It is difficult to estimate precisely how much court time the Kidd case took; the days or part-days can be counted, but the judge handled other matters on the same days, and an exact fraction would be difficult to estimate. The number of days and part-days was at least fifty-eight, and we may assume that somewhere between two and three months of the judge's year went to this matter.

Court administration in Phoenix is fairly economical; our salaries are too low. But even so, it costs approximately $60,000 a year to run a court division. Whether the time spent is regarded as a sixth or a quarter of the judge's year, the cost to the community was $10,000 to $15,000 in hard cash. But the cost to the community indirectly was the loss of the judge's time to tend to other business for the same period. Everyone else was put back a little in his law business while we stopped to examine the dentist's cord of light.

I do not believe that in our social order we can afford the luxury of letting an individual tax his fellow citizens by $10,000 or $15,000 because of a bizarre notion of how to dispose of his property. Kidd's desire to have the soul explored after his death can only be satisfied by inconveniencing everybody else who cannot have his business tended to while these decisions are being made, and Kidd's request is simply not socially important enough or valuable enough to warrant that degree of inconvenience to others. Had miner Kidd seen fit to dispose of his money before he died, he could have achieved this result without either spending the community's money or inconveniencing anyone else.

Of course I choose the Kidd illustration only because it is symptomatic of a problem. Demonstrably, the country's legal system is being called upon to carry more of a load than it is capable of carrying. One answer to the problem of court congestion is to increase and speed up productivity. But another answer that will also serve is to reduce the size of the job to be done. We have great national experience with this. Prior to the Certiorari Act of 1925, the United States Supreme Court was years behind in its work. By virtue of that statute, giving it a discretionary jurisdiction, the Court is now absolutely current. It maintains its currency by cutting the job down to a size it can manage. By the 1925 statute, the Congress of the United States decided that the people's desire or, if you will, right to take their case to the highest court in the land would have to be sacrificed to the goal of permitting that Court to get its work done. It is the theme of this chapter that in a country of more than 200 million people, this same principle must be extended, in appropriate ways, to the trial courts; the job to be performed must be cut down to size.[2]

To this end, the doctrine I advance is that the entire body of the law should be reviewed to reduce and simplify decision points.

Let me define my key term. A lawsuit is a unit of court time. That unit in turn is made up of a whole series of subunits, each of which is a decision point. Perhaps, for ease of conception, these subunits or decision points may be regarded as cells within any physical structure. The total time of the case is the time devoted to all of the decision points. Let me illustrate with a routine personal injury case. A complaint is filed. Assume that the state requires that process be served by a person over the age of twenty-one who has been a resident for a year. Arguably, the person who served this process was not properly qualified to do so, and the defendant moves to quash the service of process. The court must then decide whether the service is good or bad. In a dollar sense, let us assume that each side puts $250 worth of time into preparation of a memorandum, affidavits, and oral presentation. The court listens for fifteen minutes, looks up a little law, and fifteen minutes later makes a ruling. At that point, two things have happened. The litigation has been loaded with a $500 cost, and thirty minutes of court time have been spent in making a decision. If the state had not had the requirement that the process server be a resident for one year and over the age of twenty-one, there would have been no issue. The $500 would not have been expended, the half hour not spent. In short, when the state created the particular requirement, it created a decision point and with it the attendant costs in time and dollars.

Let us next assume that service has been ruled good, and the defendant answers. He then files a motion for judgment on the pleadings, contending that it appears on the face of the complaint that there is no jurisdiction for want of an indispensable party. Again, memorandum, cost, time. If the state procedure had specified that the question of service and the question of parties had to come up at the same time, then there would only have been one decision point, and probably the aggregate time in disposing of the two questions, and the aggregate costs, would have been less than by the system of allowing the questions to be raised consecutively. Here it is the placing of the decision point that is controlling cost and time.

The matter continues. There is discovery by interrogatories, by depositions, and finally by requests for admissions. Let us assume that the parties are contentious, and issues arise as to each of these. If so, each of those issues will in turn be a decision point, with cost and time. If the state had no discovery system, then these decision points would not arise, and those expenditures would not be made. I trust that I am not suggesting that these would be desirable economies; I am simply illustrating the time-cost factor of each decision. The matter then comes on for trial. The parties, continuing with their high degree of contentiousness, raise all sorts of evidentiary questions—each one is a decision point, and again, each has its consequences in time terms. Some of the rulings may shorten time, and others lengthen it.

But more to the core of the thing, there is the matter of what the case is about. Let us assume that the plaintiff wishes to show negligence and proximate cause, and that the defendant wishes to show contributory negligence or, in the alternative, assumption of risk. There will then have to be decisions, appropriate in each case to their respective functions, by the judge and the jury on each of these points, and because the decisions have to be made, time must be spent in gathering the facts—*i.e.*, presenting the evidence—necessary for their determination. If the jurisdiction did not have the doctrines of negligence or proximate cause as the basis of a claim for recovery, then two time elements would fall out of the case—no time would be spent in deciding these questions, and, more important, no time would be spent in proving them. If the state has abolished either the defense of contributory negligence or assumption of risk or both, then these same results will follow.

And then there is the matter of damages. If the jurisdiction is using the so-called split trial, letting the jury determine first whether there is any liability on the part of the defendant before passing on the question of damages, then the damages decision point is eliminated, with its attendant time and cost consequences in terms of proof, paying the experts, putting on the case, and deciding the issue. Again, to suggest that time could be saved is not necessarily to suggest that the saving is desirable.

The next area of decision will involve what instructions to give the jury, and here the judge will be called on to make many decisions, for he must pass on each instruction. If the jurisdiction has instructions settled in advance by publication, then there is no real decision point—one simply gives the routine auto accident instructions. If the practice is to give instructions tailored to the particular case, then there is again the time and the cost of coming to a determination on each one. After the matter is over, there will be a motion for a new trial; again, if the state did not have a new trial practice, the decision would not be made and the costs would not be borne.

The case, then, is a unit of time, which in turn is a collection of subunits of decision points. If the state should take the extreme position that it is not going to have auto accident cases heard in its courts at all, then this whole spectrum of decision points will disappear from the court load. But short of such herculean remedies, every element of the substantive law and every element of procedure creates decision points that affect costs and affect time. It follows that a tightening, or reduction of the number or complexity of these decision points—and please note that the restriction could be of either number or complexity—will reduce the size of that particular cell, or extinguish it entirely, and that the effect of this reduction will be to reduce the whole time of the case. To the extent that there is a time reduction, other business can be done in the time thus saved.

What is happening in the course of the law is an almost endless increase in the number of decision points, usually without much regard to the consequences the increase will have on the legal system. If I may use a fanciful illustration, think of the elephant in a circus, standing with feet close together upon a small supporting pedestal. Let the elephant be the collection of decision points, and the pedestal be the legal system that has to make the decisions. What happens is that the elephant grows and grows and grows as he absorbs more and more decision points. Occasionally some are taken away, as for example if my hypothetical state should eliminate the process server requirement we have discussed, but the general trend is to enlarge. The enlargement comes in two primary ways. First, the law itself grows. Second, there are more people presenting matters that need to be decided. The combined effect is that at some point, the weight of the elephant collapses the pedestal.

I am suggesting that this process must be reversed; that the elephant must grow smaller, that the volume of decision points, and hence of time, must be reduced. For convenience of discussion, let me analyze methods of doing this from three interrelated standpoints. Method number one is the reduction of jurisdiction, simply cutting out of the legal system whole areas of decision points. This is in effect what the United States Supreme Court has done with the aid of the Certiorari Act—it simply rejects nine tenths of the cases tendered to it. With due regard for the difference in structure, jurisdiction may be altered so that in effect trial courts will be doing the same thing. Second, in areas that are kept within the jurisdiction of courts, the substantive law can be altered so as to reduce the number of decision points that need to be passed upon to reach a result. For example, in the case just given, if the state eliminates the defense of assumption of risk as a matter of substantive law, whether for better or for worse, at least it will present no decision point; or if it requires that defects of process and defects of parties be considered together, there will be one less decision point.

Related to this is a third method of eliminating decision points by changing the ways in which the law performs its services. Such changes, as will be developed in a moment, can be fairly radical, but to stay within the structure of the illustration given, the existing procedure on interrogatories is that if someone wishes to object to an interrogatory, he must go to court to present his objection, thus in every instance creating a decision point. It is now proposed to alter that method of procedure so that the objecting party will merely notify his adversary that he objects and give his reason. Then if his adversary wishes to compel him to answer, the adversary will go to court. Almost certainly, the adversary will wish to insist on some occasions, but not on all: in some instances he will not think the matter worth the bother or will be persuaded by the objection made. To the extent therefore that this private exchange reduces the volume of interrogatories that must be considered in court, there will have been a reduction in the number of decision points.

JURISDICTION: HEREIN LARGELY
OF AUTOMOBILES

Law as administered by the courts is fundamentally a social service. It is a dispute-settling function of the state, and as such is on the order of delivering the mail or furnishing school lunches. It is much older than most other social services, and more important than most, but it is a social service all the same. As such, it deserves to be under constant review to determine whether in some particular it is worth either the cost or the difficulty of providing it.[3] With the best will in the world for all of its inhabitants, the state may nonetheless not be able to build a paved highway to every last farmhouse within its jurisdiction. Indeed, both the farmers and the householders may have to conform to a pre-existing road system.

For the courts, jurisdiction is the road system. The first question with every case is whether it can get to court at all. I am suggesting that we close some roads. For illustration, the law of wills may be too generous in what it will decide, in the decision points it will tackle. In Kidd's case the alternative to listening to the lady with the hair dryer and the invisible cord to heaven would be to treat the will as void and let the property escheat to the state, or pass to the heirs as if there had been no will. That decision could have been made summarily. The result would have been a one-decision-point case instead of an enormous tax on time and dollars. The court might have narrowed its jurisdiction, holding that it is no function of the courts to find an appropriate charity to which to give Mr. Kidd's money. The community can say to the spirit of Mr. Kidd, "We are sorry, but you couldn't make up your mind in life, and we are not going to undertake to make it up for you in death."

I choose the Kidd case for its color, but obviously the number of such episodes is too small to be of any real consequence. If there is to be a major reduction of the business of the courts, it must come in the treatment of auto accident cases.

The breakdown is cars. There are more than 13 million automobile accidents a year in the United States.* Many of

---

* In a message to Congress on February 6, 1968, President Johnson said "Every motorist, every passenger, and every pedestrian is affected by auto insurance—yet the system is overburdened and unsatisfactory."

these do not result in lawsuits; of 220,000 persons injured in auto accidents in New York City in 1961, 70 per cent retained a lawyer, 35 per cent filed suit, but only about 7,000 or 3.2 per cent of the whole number of cases came to trial. Forty-three per cent were not compensated at all, 10 per cent recovered less than the cost of the accident, 47 per cent recovered their full loss. Accident litigation accounts for about 65 to 80 per cent of all of the civil court cases in the United States.[4]

The figure just given is misleading in the sense that although the auto accident cases undoubtedly are *filed* in the percentage stated, so large a proportion are settled that it is not necessarily an accurate reflection of the proportion of trials. Astonishingly, there are no national statistics on the proportion of auto accident trials to all trials. However, figures available show that the accident proportion is high. For example, in Baltimore, Maryland, in a recent year, out of 1,143 trials, 541 were automobile cases. In Michigan, in one block of 2,500 cases there were 800 auto accident trials and 1,700 of all other civil cases. In Newark, New Jersey, out of 577 trials, 236 were auto negligence and 341 were all other civil.[5] Moreover, the fact that the proportion of actual trials is less than the proportion of filings does not mean that even the settled cases have no effect in clogging the calendar. Much time is lost in motions, discovery, and

This view contributed to S. J. Res. 129, adopted by the Congress in 1968, directing a comprehensive standard of the compensation system for motor vehicle licensing by the Secretary of Transportation. As was reported in the hearing on that matter before a subcommittee of the Committee on Commerce of the United States Senate, Ninetieth Congress, Second Session, Serial No. 90–60, 1966–67, traffic deaths were about 53,000, and 1.9 million suffered disabling injuries. Medical expenses were $600 million, wage losses were $2.6 billion, and property losses were $3.3 billion. Automobile insurance premiums advanced from $2.6 billion in 1950 to $9.2 billion in 1966 (Hearings, p. 12).

calendar problems for the settled cases as well. Reverting to the Baltimore figures, filings in a given year were 10,000 law cases of which 5,000 were motor vehicle, so that motor vehicle filings were 50 per cent and motor vehicle trials were about 48 per cent. Either is too high.

On this subject, I have nothing new to say; I can only join others. Clearly, any major reform of American legal procedure and administration must affect auto cases. But before we may consider changes, we must appraise the value of the system itself. The social service of the community in relation to auto accidents is that after accidents have occurred, the community distributes the loss through its legal procedures. That is, assuming the simplest situation of a two-car, two-person accident, with some property damage and some personal injury on both sides, the loss must fall somewhere. The court can charge the whole cost to Driver *A*, it can charge the whole cost to Driver *B*, it can in some fashion divide the loss between them, or it can simply wash its hands of the matter and leave the loss where it is. There are other social services the state can perform in relation to the entire auto accident problem, as for example, reducing the number of accidents by improved safety devices, driver education, and so on. And there are other postaccident social services that can be performed, such as medical services. But the sole social service I shall discuss here is that of distributing the loss, because this is all that directly involves the courts.

Before we tinker with the legal system, let us appraise the quality of the service. The basic question is, does the state at the present time perform this social service well? Have we here a system of machinery that, because of the excellence of its operations and its results, deserves preserving?

The answer must be a resounding No. It is a terrible system. It operates in an absolutely barbarous fashion. It is inefficient, incompetent, unjust, and puts an overwhelming premium on character deterioration and perjury. It is doubtful that an ingenious mind, working full time, could devise a worse method of solving this particular problem.

No more must be said about the lethargy of the system; the statistical illustrations in the first chapter need not be repeated here. In the big, controverted cases—the very areas in which speedy decision is the most needed for the sake of the human beings involved—the system is at its slow-moving worst.*

The costs are appalling. Let me emphasize hard, so that these remarks cannot be taken out of context, that they contain no want of respect for either the plaintiffs' or the defendants' bar; I am on occasion with each, though more often with the defense, and the able protagonists for each group deserve the complete respect of the bar. The plaintiffs' lawyers' national group, the American Trial Lawyers Association, until recently headed by the very responsible

* Ralph A. Petrarca, Insurance Commissioner, State of Rhode Island, at the hearings on S. J. Res. 129, *supra*, p. 37:

> In 1968, thousands of Americans will be pushed to the brink of financial ruin because of the interminable period of time which elapses between the time of the accident and the eventual court decision. Those who can no longer wait often capitulate and settle for something less than their economic losses. Those who go the full route often find that the reconstruction of events which took place three and four years ago is an impossible task. In these latter cases, the temptation to bend the truth and even to lie outright often becomes overwhelming in the desperate attempt to recover for the staggering losses of income and medical expenses. Mind you, these are basically honest citizens trapped in the cycle of our present automobile insurance system.

Mr. Sam Langerman of Phoenix, was one of the foremost organizations pushing for auto safety legislation, and in 1968 was deeply engaged in developing proposals to reduce the number of court cases.

It is inherent in a bad system that a man who suffers the loss of both legs and one arm in an auto accident must, under our system, take his damages for one arm and one leg in exchange for lost benefits for himself and his family; the value of the other leg goes for the lawyer who gets him paid for the first two amputations. This is the practical operation of the one-third contingent fee system.

This condition is, I repeat, inherent in the system. The attorney has the matter on his hands for so many years, and must handle so many minor and unsuccessful matters in order to get a success, that these economic consequences are imperative in this system: "Cutting a fat hog," we lawyers commonly say of the big verdict three-limb cases; but these are not hogs, they are people, and people shouldn't be treated this way. On the defense side as well, the costs of the system are inescapably high; here we operate on an hourly rate rather than on a contingent fee, so that the particular cases are not so spectacular, but leveled out, the results are similar.* By way of overall economic comparison, $2.20 is paid for auto accident insurance for every dollar actually paid into the hands of the injury victim. Group health programs of the Blue Cross and Blue Shield type cost $1.07 for a dollar's worth of benefits, and Social Security costs about $1.02 for a dollar's worth of benefits.

Even at this level, many persons will find it difficult to

* Insurance companies' administrative costs were $3.5 billion in 1966. Hearings, S.J. Res. 129. As the same hearings showed, the rising costs may nonetheless cause insurance companies to operate at a loss.

get topflight legal service for reasons of plain economic impossibility. One of America's foremost accident attorneys, who prefers anonymity, gives me this analysis:

(a) In the medical malpractice field, we reject all cases in which we believe the damages are likely to be less than $10,000 and we only accept cases in the $10,000–$25,000 category if we believe the negligence is gross or flagrant. Partly because of this and partly because of these cases, we accept only about one in every ten medical malpractice cases offered to us.

(b) In the products liability and slip and fall fields, we attempt to avoid processing cases with estimated damages of less than $5,000, and cases between $5,000–$15,000 must be unusually good ones before we will accept them.

(c) We try to divide the automobile accident cases into these general categories: (1) Excellent liability, (2) Good liability, (3) Average liability, (4) Mediocre liability and (5) Slim liability.

In the excellent liability category, we will accept cases with estimated values as low as $1,500. Obviously, all of these become economically very unprofitable if they have to be tried or processed through extensive discovery. Fortunately, a substantial majority can be settled without suit or shortly after the suit is filed.

With respect to cases of only "good" liability, we would be reluctant to handle one in which the estimated damages were less than $2,500. Most of these cases, too, are settled without suit or in the early stages of suit, but enough of them require discovery procedures and other pretrial preparation to make it necessary to eliminate the smaller cases.

With respect to group (3), the "average liability"

case, we would hope to avoid any of these which did not have an estimated value of at least $4,000–5,000. We would try to avoid the "mediocre liability" case" unless its estimated value was at least $5,000–7,000, and we will invariably reject the slim liability case unless it has at least a $10,000 value.

The money cost by itself would not be so serious—it's only money—if the results were reasonably speedy and were rational. But they are not only not speedy, they are not rational. The very underlying premises of the legal system on which the compensation is based are themselves obsolete and incapable of just administration even on their own terms. Let me touch these matters separately.

The underlying theory of auto accident compensation is that the loss should be borne by the person who is at fault; the central conception is one of moral liability.[6]

Whatever merit the fault theory may have had as a matter of moral punishment in a different age, insurance makes it obsolete. In a typical instance, the alleged "wrongdoer" is not punished for his "fault" in any way at all; the judgment is paid by his insurance carrier, who sets premiums that in fact are paid by the entire community. In this fashion the loss is distributed over the whole community. Apart from incidental losses, the most serious of which is the possible loss of his insurance policy, the asserted wrongdoer suffers only the same losses as the allegedly innocent victim in terms of court time, depositions, and the general nuisance of litigation.

But the system is in any case obsolete. Here, as in the immediately preceding discussion, I follow the thinking of Professors Harper and James,[7] that in our times it is the object of social insurance to protect individuals "from the consequences of pecuniary loss through such vicissitudes of life as accident, old age, sickness, and unemployment. The chief pecuniary losses are destruction of earning power and the expenses of medical care and cure and rehabilitation. Under these schemes, such losses are met (or partly met) without regard to questions of personal fault in causing them, and are distributed over a wide segment of society."

What I am saying, and what many others have said, is that given the approach of our portion of the twentieth century to human misfortune, fault is simply irrelevant to the determination of how loss shall be borne in the community. To take an extreme case, assume two essentially identical wage earners, each driving the same kind of car, with essentially interchangeable homes, with families of the same size and ages, with all factors as nearly the same in their lives as may plausibly be supposed. These twins of the automobile age collide at a street corner. By an odd quirk, their injuries are virtually identical, and each will have roughly the same medical bills and a total loss of income for a two-year period. If the income of the head of the family is cut off, the four children of each of the drivers will be identically hungry. Yet under the fault system, one should be well compensated for the misfortune and the other should have nothing. One has his doctor bills paid, and the other can be put out of the hospital for inability to pay the bill and left to recover as best he can. It is simply absurd to make the difference depend on which car entered the intersection first.

Negligence as a social rule for the distribution of loss is bad enough, but contributory negligence adds its own complications. Assume that Car A and Car B approach each other on the highway. Car A strays over the center line, smashing into the side of Car B. There can be no doubt of the negligence of A, and so of his "fault." But assume further that B was driving too fast, and that the technical consequence of his speed is that a blow that might merely have ruined his car tosses him into a ditch. He may then be denied recovery because of contributory negligence, so we reach the morally pure but socially indefensible result that, both parties having been injured and both cars having been ruined, no one is responsible for the loss; the faults cancel each other out, and therefore there is no recovery on either side. I take the example from the leading work, the *Restatement (Second) of Torts*; it could really be so. Then there is a whole mystery concerning proximate cause—was the negligence really responsible for the accident? Hence there are decision points on whether it was the crossing of the line by Car A or the speed of Car B which "really" caused the unhappy result. This can be complicated by all of the numerous other refinements that come into the question of fault, such as whether the risk was assumed, whether the suffering party really had a chance to get out of the way, and so on.

In the preceding paragraphs, I have suggested that in a social view of the distribution of loss, all of the questions that we have just been posing are immaterial and ought to be regarded as obsolete; they are not worth asking. But up to that point in the discussion, we had assumed that, whether they were worth asking or not, they were at least capable of being answered truthfully.

But this is not at all so. This is all too often a search for truth that is both as ceremonial and as profitable as reading the tea leaves or analyzing the entrails of an ox. The whole process, from beginning to end, may be the purest mumbo jumbo.

Assume that an auto accident happened at the corner of

Forty-second Street and Seventh Avenue in New York City
on July 1, 1962. The driver of one or another of two cars
either did or didn't go too quickly, either did or didn't go
against the light, either did or didn't notice a hand signal.
The entire episode of human experience, from the moment
of approach to the moment of collision, took two or three
seconds. The resultant lawsuit was promptly filed, and now
in 1968, the matter comes on for trial. The drivers, the
passengers, and conceivably some street corner witnesses are
all supposed to tell under oath five years or more after the
event precisely what happened so long ago in two or three
seconds, and this with respect to matters that no human being would have been at all likely to have noticed with par-
ticularity even at the time. Their memories are necessarily
hopelessly faded, and what is left is colored by their interest.
As James Marshall develops in his useful work on psychology and the law, no one can possibly tell what actually happened in many auto accidents.[8] In this process we are tying
up the entire legal system of the United States hopelessly,
and we are doing it

1. By looking for answers to questions not worth asking.
2. By asking questions that cannot possibly be truthfully or accurately answered except by accident.
3. At the cost of making it impossible to carry on the
   rest of the social service of dispute settling.

Any system with these results needs a fresh look. Personally, I would extinguish the entire mass of these decision
points by totally revising the law of accidents so that it
would no longer be necessary to deal with negligence, contributory negligence, proximate cause, or assumption of

risk. There are various ways of solving the problem, and I do not need for the purpose of these lectures to make up my mind among them, but some plan I would surely adopt. Specifically:

(1) We might completely shift the nature of automobile insurance and adopt instead the principles of fire insurance. The normal automobile insurance is carried to insure the individual against claims by others—I carry my automobile insurance so that if I hit someone else and he sues me, he can be paid. My fire insurance is of course totally different; I carry that so that if there is a fire, I can be paid. We might abolish the law of negligence and provide that each person should carry his own automobile insurance as he does his fire insurance.

(2) We might move the entire mass of auto accident cases out of the courts into some kind of administrative agency with decision-making powers. This, by itself, seems to me to have no virtue at all unless the standards by which the administrative agency passes on the accidents are totally changed. To move negligence cases to some other agency is simply to give a court another name.

(3) If, on the other hand, we eliminate the standard of negligence, then the administrative agency may be very serviceable; it might function as do compensation commissions in relation to industrial accidents. If the workman is injured on the job, he receives compensation regardless of fault: he does not have to account for why he lost a hand; it is enough that he lost it. Nonetheless, someone must determine what he has coming if he and his employer's insurer do not agree.

(4) The leading automobile accident plan proposes that up to $10,000 for economic loss and up to $5,000 for pain and suffering would be paid by one's own insurer, leaving

only the larger cases to go to the courts under the traditional rules of negligence, contributory negligence, and so on. This, with much elaboration, is the proposal of Professor Robert Keeton of Harvard, and Professor Jeffrey O'Connell of the University of Illinois for a "basic protection plan." Another plan, with important variations from the Keeton-O'Connell plan and more modest benefits, is in use in the Province of Saskatchewan. The Keeton-O'Connell plan has been approved by one house of the Massachusetts State Legislature and was introduced in 1967 in five other states.[9]

(5) A still further variant might be a government program like Medicare—such proposals are disparaged as Autocare, but this label can also be worn with honor—whereby the cost of auto loss would be borne from taxation, perhaps like Social Security, again without any reference whatsoever to fault factors. No one has suggested that the sixty-five-year-old who slips and falls should have to prove that he was innocent of walking too quickly before Medicare will pay his hospital bills, and there is no good ground for imposing any stiffer standard as a result of an accident in a moving vehicle.

I am aware that, in taking up this subject, I enter a well-plowed field.

One of the fathers of the reform is Professor Albert Ehrenzweig of the University of California Law School at Berkeley, author of a slight and extremely provocative volume.[10] Very extensive work has been done by Professor Alfred F. Conrad and others at Michigan.[11] All work takes a lead from a 1932 Columbia University study.[12] Clearly, we are dealing with no novel thought in general, although equally clearly, there is room for sharp difference about particulars. There are strenuous criticisms of the Keeton-O'Connell plan.[13]

Professor Harry Kalven at the University of Chicago

argues that court congestion is not really a problem in the United States outside of New York, Philadelphia, Boston, and Chicago. Morally, he endorses the fault principle.[14] For reasons developed throughout these lectures, I think him wrong on both points; he is surely not taking into account our next 100 million people.

The Defense Research Institute argues that the Keeton-O'Connell plan is actuarially unsound and that it presents financial difficulties inadequately considered.[15] Mr. James S. Kemper, Jr., head of the Kemper Insurance Group, makes other substantial and temperate criticisms, which require consideration.[16]

The argument has also been made from independent sources that the particular plan may increase lawsuits and increase fraud.

The argument is earnestly made that if the abolition of fault is good for auto accidents, the principle should be extended to all other wrongs; and that if the system is good up to $10,000, why should it not be equally good over this figure? These latter contentions seem to me captious. The law is used to the notion that not all fires can be put out at once.

In these chapters, I propose an agenda for further discussion rather than attempting to draft a final bill. Hence, I duck the details of the Keeton-O'Connell plan and content myself with embracing the proposition that long before the 300 millionth American is born something drastic must be done.[17] At a minimum, I would adopt the proposal of the Arden House Session of the American Assembly in 1965 as another *Recommendation*:

10. "New measures must be devised to assure prompt relief to hundreds of thousands of automobile accident

victims and to reduce court delays caused by the press
of personal injury litigation. Remedial devices to accomplish these ends should be thoroughly explored,
among them: 1. eliminating the fault principle in
determining liability in most automobile accident personal injury cases; 2. the 'basic protection plan'
whereby the first $10,000 of loss would be recovered
on an insurance basis; and 3. the establishment of
machinery for administrative compensation, as in industrial accidents."

Chief Justice Warren has never addressed himself, so far
as I know, to the auto accident subject, but I borrow his
spirit in his sentence, "In a century which has been characterized by growth and modernization in science, technology
and economics, the legal fraternity is still living in the past."
There is no more vivid illustration than auto accidents. Our
automotive engineers have been able to give us vehicles
with which we can cover the land. Our highway engineers
have been able to give us the roads and highways on which
to do it. There are car defects and road bottlenecks; no one
brags about the Long Island Expressway system at rush
hour. But our profession has failed frightfully to deal with
the one share of this transportation system that has been
entrusted to us, the distribution of the losses caused by its
operation; the legal system is stalled permanently on the
Long Island Expressway at rush hour. The Model T and
the country road as serious methods of transportation are
extinct. We must, simply imperatively must, now create our
own superhighway for the accident cases.* I like the Arden

* This is not simply a reformer's point of view. See, for example, the
statement of the Insurance Company of North America, in Hearings,
S. J. Res. 129, *supra*, p. 147: "What is needed is an entirely new approach to the problems presented by victims of automobile accidents—

House proposal particularly because it adds to the Keeton-O'Connell plan a proposal for administrative procedure.

"COMPLEXITY": THE EXPANSION OF DECISION POINTS

Let me come back to the symbol of the ever-growing elephant on the small pedestal. This was the figure suggested earlier for the expansion of decision points beyond the capacity of the system to cope with their determination. I would like to demonstrate the lack of consideration by the lawmaking portion of the legal system for the law-administering portion, with the result that the law grows, heedless of its administrative consequences. Until this point, I have been talking principally about time consumption; here I would also consider dollar costs. We may take as a starting point the question proposed by Professor Ben Kaplan, in a comparison of American and German procedure: "Are we in this country simply paying too much in time, effort, and money to pursue the finer lineaments of truth which must in any event elude us?"[18]

The problem here considered is particularly familiar in American administrative law. Beginning in the first half of the nineteenth century, reform legislatures constantly observed social evils, passed corrective legislation, and then usually failed to realize that nothing was happening, that their administrative machinery was totally inadequate for translation of the goal or standard into action.[19] The law-

---

an approach that would harmonize with the thinking and needs of our automobile-oriented society." This was developed in a thoughtful address by Bradford Smith, Jr., chairman of the board of that company, who said that without "corrective measures," the future of automobile accident insurance as a private enterprise was in danger. Id. at 154.

maker was heedless of law administration. We are no longer so unsophisticated; but the administrative consequences of a law change are still not where they belong, in the bright center of our vision. This requires demonstration in some detail.

Procedure

Let me take for analysis a recent change in Rule 23 of the Federal Rules of Civil Procedure.[20] This rule, dealing with the circumstances in which one or more persons can represent a large group, has been the poorest rule on the books and needed a complete rewrite, which it has had; but incidental to the rewrite has appeared a boundless proliferation of decision points costly in both time and dollars.

Previously, some class actions had been binding on the whole class; others had not. In the revision, the decision was made to eliminate from the world of class actions entirely those which would not be binding on the whole class —if the suit was to be a class action at all, then the final judgment would be binding on all persons in the class, whether they were in the case or not, except for certain circumstances that I may here put aside.

If this matter is to be understood, we must go through each complexity a step at a time:

Had it been decided to confine the new class actions to those that earlier had been in a category that might have been binding on the class, most of our problems would not arise. But Section 23 (b)(3) was put in to provide that there might also be a class action when six—count them—six overlapping decision points are determined. There may be a class action where (1) "the court finds that the questions of law or fact common to the members of the class predom-

inate over any questions affecting only individual members";
(2) in addition "a class action" must be "superior to other
available methods for the fair and efficient adjudication of
the controversy." Then follow the overlapping matters per-
tinent to those findings. The court is to consider (3) the
interest of members of the class in individually controlling
the prosecution or defense of separate actions; (4) the extent
and nature of any litigation concerning the controversy already commenced by or against members of the class; (5)
the desirability or undesirability of concentrating the litigation of the claims in the particular forum; (6) the difficulties likely to be encountered in the management of a
class action.

And when are these matters to be considered? "As soon
as practicable after the commencement of an action brought
as a class action, the court shall determine by order whether
it is to be so maintained." But that judgment is not final—
it can be reconsidered. Moreover, there is one other step
specially created for suits of the type just described—in any
of these cases "the court shall direct to the members of the
class the best notice practicable under the circumstances,
including individual notice to all members who can be identified through reasonable efforts." Various consequences follow from the notice.

The practical effect of all of this structure is that so many
decision points have been created, and so cumbersome a procedure is necessarily involved in determining them, that for
practical purposes we have put a lawsuit in front of a lawsuit; and it is not two for the price of one. Some poor soul,
unaware of the pitfalls, starts a Section 23(b)(3) class action.
He wants to have at the defendant. But before battle can
be joined, and "as soon as practicable," the court has to
make findings. These findings may very well involve the

taking of evidence; the matter of the relative interest of members of the class might perfectly well be a highly factual matter. Most basically, whether the questions of law and fact are truly "common to the members of the class" or whether they are quite uncommon, may depend upon all sorts of factual details.

This is no flight of fancy;[21] I recently went through my first case under the new rule. A small trade association composed of roughly 10 per cent of the members of a particular industry brought an action on behalf of all persons engaged in that industry to litigate the validity of a particular state action. The state defendants objected to the suit as a class action and demanded a determination "as soon as practicable," asking for the taking of evidence. Thereupon, as would appear to be quite appropriate under the requirement, the matter was set for hearing, but before it could be heard, depositions had to be taken from absent witnesses at a point more than one hundred miles away. When the matter came on for hearing, witnesses not only came from the locale of the court but also came from two different points, traveling at least one hundred miles.

The testimony developed from the stand and on the depositions raised grave doubts as to whether this was an appropriate case for a class action. On the substantive point at issue, even the members of the trade association did not themselves all have a common position; and it also developed from live testimony that large contractors had a substantially different economic interest from small contractors and that nonunion contractors had a very different interest from union contractors. In short, there was very great room to doubt that there were really "questions of law or fact common to the members of the class" as there were claimed to be.

Nonetheless a trial judge, laboring with his first case under the new rule, heard the evidence, considered the briefs and the arguments, and ruled that this was a suitable class case. Thereupon, the state, using an extraordinary writ procedure, applied for what amounts to an interlocutory appellate review in the state Court of Appeals. That court, by its order, indicated that the rule had not been complied with and that the matter could not proceed as a class action. The case then returned to the trial court, where the plaintiff amended to make the suit an individual action.

The plaintiff was thus in the position legally it would have been in had it never sought the class action in the first place. And yet the economic position was not at all the same. The plaintiff had exhausted the funds available to battle this particular matter. It was forced to yield to a settlement that it would never have accepted but for the exhaustion. A month later, another matter came along, wholly unrelated, of concern to the same small trade association; this matter it had to pass entirely until its treasury could be built up again.

Let me not exaggerate. None of this involved much money or much time. A trial court lost approximately two days of court time and an appellate court lost about half a day; many miles were traveled, depositions taken, research done, and briefs written. The parties spent some thousands of dollars in counsel fees plus an indeterminate amount of time with state officials. It was all waste, all aimless, all tying up court time and dissipating client dollars; the case didn't need to be a class action to begin with. It was expensive education. If these six new overlapping decision points had never been created, if this type of class action had never been put into the rules at all, the parties might have got on with the business they had.

Putting these refinements into the law weights the system terribly in favor of the party with the long purse. A defendant determined to make a plaintiff jump the hurdles of every last decision point may well exhaust the resources of the plaintiff; in the interest of perfection, we run the risk of pricing justice out of the market.

Let me not leave the subject of the rules with any suggestion that they are generally open to the criticism just made. They are not; for the most part they eliminate, not create, decision points. The provisions of Rule 8 concerning pleading, settling for "a short and plain statement of the claim" has gone far to eliminate the endless wrangling over whether the pleading was adequate. The recent amendments to Rule 12, which require that many defenses be bundled together and presented at one time, cut down on decisions in series. The amendment of Rule 25 concerning substitution of parties will largely eliminate decisions as to whether the right public officer is named in a case. For one concrete illustration of what can be done, Rule 12(b) specifies that in the appropriate circumstances a motion to decide the case may properly be treated either as a motion to dismiss or as a motion for summary judgment. Thus eliminated is an entire decision area that formerly involved the question of how the motion was to be treated. All these things cut down, all of them speed the course of justice; my isolated criticisms should not diminish the attitude of general enthusiasm for the rules. But they do give rise to a *Recommendation:*

> 11. All rules or statutes governing procedure should be carefully analyzed to ensure that their application will not take undue court time or add to the cost of litigation. The presumption in favor of economy and speed is rebuttable where fairness is at stake, but it is a strong presumption all the same.

The Commercial Code
and Its Decision Points

The Uniform Commercial Code does not need my enthusiasm, and it has my respect. It is clearly the most immense piece of commercial legislation ever undertaken, a great product both of the American Law Institute and the Uniform Law Commissioners; it more than takes the place of the seven uniform acts that had preceded it. The act undertook "to simplify, clarify and modernize the law governing commercial transactions," as well as to make the law uniform and to permit continued expansion of commercial practices. Although the act did not set out to create additional decision points, and thus give the courts added work to do, some of its sections have that consequence; others move in the direction of reducing the court load.

Section 2-302 deals with "unconscionable" provisions in contracts. The section expressly provides that if the court finds a contract or any of its clauses "to have been unconscionable at the time it was made" the court may either refuse to enforce the contract or limit its application. Under the previous law, this was done essentially by judicial intuition. Illustrative cases given within the code section are the case of a clause limiting time for complaints over a shipment of catsup when the defects could be discovered only by microscopic analysis; or a case in which a used car was delivered instead of a new one and in which the contract contained language that if strictly applied would nullify the right to receive a new car, and many others.

Intuitive unfairness may be the fastest method of determining the point, but the reality of the unfairness may depend on evidence; if the transaction is a commercial matter in an area of business in which the court is not acquainted, there may be arguments for or against a contract provision that arises from the facts of the trade of which the court, unless instructed, would be ignorant. Hence, the drafters of Section 2-302 created for its operation a new decision point and provided for the taking of evidence in cases of this kind. Section 2-302(2) provides:

> When it is claimed or appears to the court that the contract or any clause thereof may be unconscionable the parties shall be afforded a reasonable opportunity to present evidence as to its commercial setting, purpose and effect to aid the court in making the determination.

Clearly this will, and is intended to, put a new sublawsuit into a major lawsuit. In the catsup case, without this provision, the sole facts to be determined by evidence would have been whether there was an agreement to deliver catsup, whether the catsup was delivered, and whether the complaint was made within the requisite time. Such proof would be a matter of two or three documents at most—all of the facts might well be admitted. But with this new decision point in the case, evidence must now be taken to determine such matters as how quickly defects ought to be discovered in catsup, what the shifts of the market are and the resultant fairness or unfairness of allowing belated complaints, what the problems of spoilage may be, what degree of caution a reasonable catsup dealer would exercise upon receipt of the product, and so on. What could have been a few minutes' case may then become a very complex, time-consuming, and expensive one; certainly some expert testimony will be needed.

Let me stress again that by giving the example, I am merely noting the proliferation of litigation, not expressing a view as to whether this particular extension is or is not desirable; in all candor, I don't know. One may assume that the clause was drafted with consideration of the added demand it would make on court time; or was it?

Section 9-313 is a good example of a failure on the part of the drafters to eliminate a troublesome, existing decision point. Subsection 1 provides, with exclusions immaterial here, that the question of whether and when goods become fixtures is to be determined by the law of the particular state.

The practical consequence of this provision is to leave it to the laws of the fifty states as to what is a fixture; there is no uniform rule on this point except that there is uniform nonuniformity. Many states have no clearly defined law of fixtures. The practical consequence is that when this issue is reached in a case, a court will have to take briefs and arguments on matters that might have been avoided altogether if the statute had provided a rule of its own. This was apparently an oversight.

> The draftsmen of the Code assumed that . . . Section 7 of the Uniform Conditional Sales Act (UCSA) had worked satisfactorily . . . ; that no fundamental reconsideration was necessary; and that, except for remedying . . . one deficiency . . . the problem was simply to redraft and clarify the solutions of the UCSA and to integrate them into the Code. How wrong we were![22]

Although the articles do not deal solely with the failure to define fixtures, the Commercial Code bibliographies (1966 and 1967), prepared by Mitchell J. Ezer for the Joint Committee on Continuing Legal Education of the American Law Institute and the American Bar Association, list thirteen articles dealing with fixtures under the Uniform Commercial

Code. Clearly, there will be considerable litigation as a result of Section 9-313.

A decision point creator that must be labeled unfortunate, but perhaps inescapable, is Section 9-504(3). This part of the secured transactions section of the statute deals with the power of a secured party to sell collateral after a default. Assume for example, that the creditor has loaned money to a dealer to procure a dozen pianos and is granted a security interest in the pianos. The dealer is unable to pay, and the creditor repossesses. He now wishes to sell the pianos and recover his funds, and the problem is how to do it. This section says that "every aspect of the disposition including the method, manner, time, place and terms must be commercially reasonable." Some definition of this phrase is given in Section 9-507(2)—the sale will be regarded as commercially reasonable if it is sold "in the usual manner in any recognized market therefor"; but what is the recognized market for a block of twelve pianos? The transaction may be commercially reasonable if "sold in conformity with reasonable commercial practices among dealers in the type of property sold," but what are they? In the light of these uncertainties, the provision apparently contemplates that one may apply for a court order to determine that a particular method of disposition is reasonable before one makes the sale. The practical effect of this is to create a new kind of declaratory judgment proceeding, whereby the party gets an advance order—which again may involve evidence, argument, and decision—to protect himself against the uncertainties of the sale.[23] There would be less litigation if the secured creditor had been authorized to inform the debtor of the type of disposition he proposed; the burden might have been placed on the debtor to ask a court to direct the type of disposition he wanted within a period of time, or hold his peace.

The Commercial Code does not always create additional decision points; sometimes it eliminates them or at least attempts to do so. A debtor may have a whole series of secured creditors, and if he does, their rights to his limited funds may depend on their priority. Section 9-312(5) deals with priorities among conflicting security interests in the same collateral and gives priority to the first to file if all are perfected by filing. The section provides further that if one of the competing claims is perfected by some other means, as for example by taking possession, the first prevails. Since there is no mention of knowledge of a prior interest, the rule appears to remove knowledge as a relevant criterion in determining priority,[24] thus eliminating an always time-consuming decision point as to who knew what.

Conflict of Laws

We may begin our discussion of the creation of new decision points in the law of conflicts with the great case of *Babcock v. Jackson*.[25] Mr. and Mrs. Jackson, residents of Rochester, New York, left that city for a drive into Canada, taking as their guest a Miss Babcock. They swiftly crossed into the Province of Ontario; a few hours later, Mr. Jackson lost control of the car and hit a stone wall, to the great injury of Miss Babcock. When the party returned to New York, Miss Babcock sued Jackson for negligence.

It was the law of Ontario that a guest might not sue her driver. New York had no such restriction. The case therefore depended upon the rules of conflict of laws. If New York were to apply Ontario law, then there could be no recovery; if it applied its own law, the opposite result might be reached.

Under the prevailing conflicts law, the answer was simple: the controlling law is that of the place of the accident. In any given case this becomes a two-decision-point affair: where did the accident occur, and what is the law of that place?

But the rule has only simplicity to commend it. All the parties involved in the accident are New Yorkers, their lives are lived there, the social loss of their accident must be borne there; Jackson's unhappy lapse could have occurred anywhere. He might have gone farther east in New York, south to Pennsylvania, west to Ohio, or north into Canada; and it might have made no difference as to the eventual actual human result. As New York had previously observed, in modern travel, the place of the accident may be entirely fortuitous.

How, then, is the matter to be decided? The court speaks of the "contacts" of the competing jurisdictions and the parties; it speaks of the "center of gravity." But just what is supposed to be taken into account in lieu of the original decision point? What takes the place of the situs of the accident as the controlling factor? The opinion is not entirely clear. A half-dozen professors commenting on the decision in an unusual collection shortly after it was issued came to divergent conclusions;[26] for example, Professor Albert Ehrenzweig takes what seems to me legitimate comfort from the court's citation of an article of his own making the car's insurance a factor to be considered, whereas Professor Currie has taken another view.[27]

Once the court sets out to "weigh" relative state interests, it has opened up a whole additional area for decision, as to many parts of which evidence may need to be taken to ensure that there is full understanding. The factors actually taken into account by the New York court in deciding that the New York laws should prevail become a list of its decision points:

1. The parties are New Yorkers.
2. The car is garaged, licensed, and undoubtedly insured, in New York.
3. The trip originated in New York and was to end there.
4. New York has no reason not to apply its policy as between its residents merely because the accident occurred outside the state; and contrariwise, Ontario has no reason to object to what New York may do. The limit of the Ontario interest is in its defendants and its insurance carriers.
5. If the issue in the case were a different rule of the road, as for example as to speed and care of driving, a different result might be reached; Ontario does have a substantial interest in enforcing rules as to the use of its roads.

I believe this was a highly desirable change in law, but let us note its consequences for the legal process. What was a one-decision-point case, or at most two, becomes a six- or eight-decision-point case. Matters on which essentially no evidence had to be taken (the place of the accident) remain in the case; but now it becomes necessary to determine the intent of the parties with respect to their trip, the quality of their relationships to New York, and so on. For example, suppose that the trio had been planning to stay in Ontario indefinitely at the time of the accident; suppose that Miss Babcock had been a Canadian from some other province who was being taken home; suppose she had come from some other state in the United States; each of these might have made some difference. If so, as to each, the facts must be determined and the law declared.

The case illustrates that as the law improves, it is likely to grow more complex; whether for good or for ill, here is a change in law that adds just a little bit more to the burdens on courts and judges.

The American Law Institute is in the midst of a new RE-STATEMENT OF THE CONFLICT OF LAWS. One of the objects of this new RESTATEMENT is to eliminate some of the rigidities of its predecessor. I hasten to acknowledge that I personally have happily followed the lead of the reporter for this revision, Professor Willis Reese of Columbia University. And yet, I must also confess that, now that we are virtually across the stream, some misgivings occur; in the course of reducing rigidity, we have been turning out decision points like popcorn. A few illustrations will suffice.

Section 9, dealing with when a state may apply its local law to a conflict situation, says that "a court may not apply the local law of its own state to determine a particular issue unless application of this law would be reasonable in the light of the relationship of the state to the issue and to the person, thing or occurrence involved."[28]

In applying this principle, we are told that dogs must be kept muzzled in State X, but not in adjacent State Y. A lives in Y, one mile from X border. If he permits his dog to run unmuzzled and one day the dog crosses into X and there bites someone, the victim may hold A liable, applying its local law to A who let his dog run unmuzzled in a state in which it was perfectly proper for him to do so.

This may very well be reasonable in an eastern state. On the other hand, assume that the two states happen to be Utah and Colorado, and the dog is a sheep dog who is busily engaged in minding the sheep of his Utah owner. This is a duty it can perform only unmuzzled, and if this dog crosses the line into Colorado in the course of herding sheep in open range, the same result may not be so reasonable. In that context, the rule amounts to a holding that Colorado can keep a Utah rancher from having dogs to herd his sheep. I hasten to add that I do not mean to decide the point or suggest that I know what the decision should be; I do mean to suggest that applying this standard to this fact situation may result in a good deal of trial time to determine what is reasonable. Indeed, this is fully recognized by the RESTATEMENT, which says, "Whether application of a state's law would be reasonable depends upon the relationship of the state to the thing and upon the precise issue involved." This opens a broad field of inquiry as to (1) the relationship, and (2) all facts bearing on the precise issue.

The new RESTATEMENT OF CONFLICTS also makes a new start on the law of torts, reflecting the approach of *Babcock v. Jackson*. The old law had been based upon the law of the place of the wrong; the new law substitutes the standard that tort should be governed by the "law of the state which has the most significant relationship with the occurrence and with the parties." This is carried out not only for the law of auto accidents but for the entire body of tort law, so that where there had been one decision point before, an entire galaxy is now created for personal injuries, for injuries to tangible things, for defamation, for invasion of the right of privacy, and so on.[29]

The difference is illustrated by comparing the old Sections 378 and 379 with their parallel new provisions. The old sections tell us with stark simplicity that "the law of the place of wrong determines whether a person has sustained a legal injury." "The law of the place of wrong determines" whether a person is responsible for harm he deliberately caused, or harm that is unintended, or harm for which the intent is immaterial. This approach gives two questions to the court to answer—where did the wrong happen and what is the law there? The new Section 379 says that the law of the state "which has the most significant relationship with the occurrence and with the party" determines these questions. It directs the court to consider the place where the injury occurred, the place where the conduct occurred, the residence of the parties, and "the place where the relationship, if any, between the parties is centered." A variant of this is given for injuries to tangible property.

To give some idea of the complexity of the matter, consider Section 379 (c) on fraud and misrepresentation. If a buyer makes a purchase based on false representations in State *A*, every act occurring in that state, then the local law of that state would usually determine the plaintiff's rights. If the plaintiff's action in reliance on the false representation took place in a different state from that in which the representation was made, the court will consider the place or places where the buyer acted in reliance on the representation; the place where the buyer received the representation; the place where the defendant made the representation; the domicile and place of residence of the parties; the place where any tangible thing that was the subject of the transaction was located; and the place where the plaintiff was to render a performance.

The effect is to give a check list of six contacts, and could require proof, briefing, and argument on all six of them. This woeful complexity the RESTATEMENT modifies by saying that "if any two of the above-mentioned contacts, apart from the defendant's domicile, state of incorporation or place of business, are located wholly in a single state, this would usually be the state of the governing law."[30]

For another and more bizarre illustration from the tort field, take § 149, Illustration 1, of the RESTATEMENT OF CONFLICTS, as considered in 1968. This illustration deals with the choice of law where a husband and wife are domiciled in State Y. During a sojourn in State X husband slanders his wife's chastity. For some reason not apparent in the state of the record, wife sues her husband in State Z. What she was doing there and how she gets service is not explained.

The case, happily, is a rare one. In 1967, a lady named Tonsmeire sued her husband for impugning her chastity. The case occurred after the divorce, and in any event was entirely in the State of Alabama. If there is a single instance of what I may term interstate slander of chastity, it is not reflected in any reported case since 1900. The likelihood of the question arising on a three-state basis is roughly comparable to the number of times one really has to decide how many angels may dance on the point of a pin. Where hundreds of American Law Institute members gather from all over America to confront the issues of the day, this particular issue may well qualify as more intriguing than real.

But let us suppose the case arises. We begin with the probable damages. Because there are no cases of tristate, or even two-state, slander of chastity by a husband, we cannot learn from experience. We must therefore pass to intrastate slander. The only reported case of intrastate husband-wife slander is postdivorce, so to get the feel of the thing, we review all cases of slander of chastity, by anyone, in one state.

Alas, the price is low. The plain truth of the matter is that on the contemporary American scene, chastity may be (and happily is) a virtue beyond the price of rubies. But the reputation for chastity is not so priced in the courts of law. Although we find one $25,000 episode (a husband impugning the chastity of his ex-wife), the price of slander is normally considerably less: there are awards of $500 to $7,000 in the remaining cases. The most likely to be collected in any sample instance of this behavioral misdeed is about $2,500, in one state, for a slander by anyone.

The RESTATEMENT illustration does not tell us what law is to be applied in our happily remote three-state case. It does tell us what factors are to be taken into account in determining that law.

(1) We are to determine the "primary purpose" of the law of the state of domicile. Is it to punish "misconduct" or to secure "compensation"?

How do we determine this? The law is either statutory, in which case a review of the legislative history in most states, in most instances, will reveal nothing; or it is case law, in which case the purpose is probably unstated, confused, or multiple. The probable cost, in lawyer-hour time, of reaching a negative conclusion: $500 to $1,000.

(2) What is the relative weight of these factors? Because they cannot be measured, a conservative cost measure before an impatient judge is $250 for a lawyer's time.

(3) Was the purpose of the law to avoid docket clogging or harassment of parties? Cost of presenting an answer, $250.

(4) This leaves two questions. The first is the amount of taxpayer dollars to be spent in answering the foregoing questions: judge's salary, capital expense, bailiff's salary, court reporter, clerk, and so on. Surely $500 is conservative.

(5) How much cost was there to other litigants, waiting to have more substantial questions answered by the courts? The mind boggles.

(6) How much cost flows from failing to give a direct answer to a direct question of choice of law?

Answer: More than the case is worth. All that saves this bit of lawmaking from being a real drain on time and dollars through proliferation of decision points is that the case will probably never occur.[31]

The same approach is taken as to the law of contracts. Under the old view, the validity of a contract was governed by the law of the place of contract. For this has been substituted in the new Section 332 the general provision that the validity of the contract should be determined by the law of the state "with which the contract has its most significant relationship." This open end definition of validity is limited by the right of the parties to choose their own law.

This, by itself, is not of terribly great practical importance in most commercial contracts because validity is relatively rarely an issue; the real problem of a contract is its construction. Section 334(e), Tentative Draft No. 6, RESTATE-MENT OF CONFLICTS, provides that the standards for determining validity shall also govern the choice of law for construction.

We, therefore, reach the important open question: if the place of contract and the place of performance are the same state there is no real question; the law of that state prevails. But in national commerce, the place of contract is likely to be one state and the place of performance another. If so, "additional factors will be considered in determining with which [state] the contract has its most significant relationship." Six decision points that are to be taken into account by the court are:

1. The place of contract.
2. The place of performance.
3. The place of the subject matter of the contract.
4. Factors relating to the situs of the parties.

5. "The law under which the contract will be most effective."

6. The catchall for "other contacts," because "any contact which can reasonably be said to connect the contract with a given state will be considered by the courts." For example, the place "where the contract was negotiated is a contact to be considered."

The substitution of these various factors for the old hard line rule clearly adds to the burden on the courts in determining the validity of the contract or its construction. To that extent the change is a further load on judicial administration, though it may be a most worthwhile addition. These factors should not add much by way of time because almost none of them will involve the substantial taking of evidence. The factual information necessary to permit this thought process to operate comes into the record in any case without making a special effort to attain it. It will be obvious in most instances where the place of performance is or what the domicile is or where the subject matter of the contract is located. The change will expand briefing and argument and decision time by requiring further thought and discussion of these various factors, but the new elements will not require added proof time.

It would be grossly unjust to this good work to leave the impression that it is in all respects as wide open as the examples suggest. A good contrary illustration is the section on jurisdiction over things. Section 56 provides that, "A state has power to exercise judicial jurisdiction to affect interests in a thing if the relationship of the thing to the state is such as to make the exercise of such jurisdiction reasonable." At this point, we have invoked reasonableness again, with all of the problems of proof that attend when one seeks seriously to penetrate that happy haze. But ten sections follow that do specify what is to be regarded as reasonable, along with a most constructive general limitation that persons interested must have an opportunity to know of any impending legal action. It is reasonable to give a state power over land within its borders; over chattels within its borders that are not in the course of transportation; over documents within its borders; over intangibles embodied in documents within its borders, and so on. Section 65 throws in the sponge, but candidly; it provides that a state may exercise jurisdiction to affect interests in unspecified intangibles "if the relationship of the state to the thing and to the parties involved makes the exercise of such jurisdiction reasonable." Here, clearly, there could be decision points galore; the comment tells us that it is impossible to be more incisive than this because "no more definite rule may be stated at the present time because the field is largely unexplored." This, in short, is a decision point bundle that has to be left wide open for the normal development of the common law. The whole group of the conflict and commercial code provisions however lead to this *Recommendation:*

> 12. Like rules of procedure, substantive rules of law should be created with an eye to the administrative consequences of determining them.

Taxation

Let me conclude this exercise in the survey of the contemporary creation of decision points by a single illustration from the tax laws. The collapsible corporation provisions of the Internal Revenue Code illustrate the manner in which law expands itself; here is the endless rippling quality of decision points, the law first creating a problem, then creating a solution, then modifying the solution, and at each point making more numerous the points of decision.

Once the Internal Revenue Code made a distinction between ordinary income and capital gain, it necessarily opened an entire new area of legal endeavor as persons sought to manage their affairs so as to have the more favorable tax treatment. One such device was the collapsible corporation; persons engaged in the production of goods, as for example a moving picture, might establish a corporation for the manufacture, and then dissolve the corporation after the product was produced but before it was sold. The property would then be cast back upon the shareholders. Had the corporation sold the property, it would have realized ordinary income, and would then have declared a dividend; there would have been two taxes, one at the corporate ordinary income rate and the other at the individual's ordinary income rate. By this device, the individuals could sell the product and take a capital gain.[32] What followed illustrates the reproductive capacities of the law. Boy (corporation) meets girl (taxation); they merge to produce the somewhat-taxed collapsible corporation and the grandchildren are a long list of decision points, truly created from this marriage; none of them existed before.

Specifically, the Revenue Act of 1950 adopted provisions to diminish the benefits of the collapsing practice. The 1950 provisions were further amended in 1958 by Internal Revenue Code Section 341(e). These provisions are a massive body of code law; there is a rule, there are exceptions, there are exceptions to the exceptions, and there is a third tier of exceptions to the exceptions to the exceptions. A random list of a few problems suggested by Section 341 follows:

(1) A collapsible corporation is defined as a "corporation formed or availed of principally for the manufacture, construction, or production of property. . . ." The question of the "principal" purpose of a corporation requires decisions on points both of law and fact.

(2) Such corporations are those engaged in various activities before the realization "of a substantial part of the taxable income to be derived from such property," thus raising questions of what is substantial.

(3) It becomes necessary to determine what are the "341 assets" of a corporation, a technical term meaning property held for less than three years, where such property is part of the "stock in trade of the corporation" and "would properly be included in the inventory of the corporation"; it is property held "primarily for sale to customers" and "in the ordinary course of its trade or business." This of course presents the problems of what is stock in trade, what would ordinarily be included, what is primarily for sale to customers, what is ordinary trade, and so on.

(4) A series of special consequences flow from 5 per cent ownership, 20 per cent ownership, and 70 per cent ownership of interests, thus requiring a determination of these facts.

(5) A whole set of definitions is required for purposes of Subsection (e); "Subsection (e) asset" means, to quote only one subpart of the definition, "property used in the trade or business . . . but only if the unrealized depreciation on all such property on which there is unrealized depreciation exceeds the unrealized appreciation on all such property on which there is no realized appreciation."

What has been enumerated is the smallest part of the problems spawned by the collapsible corporation statute. There is no criticism implied in the example; for all I know, this is the best way of handling a problem that has to be handled. Our interest is neither the law of corporations nor the law of taxation, but rather the burdens on courts and the costs to litigants.

What has in fact happened is the creation of a modest new load for courts; there are about one hundred fifty paragraphs of holdings in the United States Code Annotated that on the one hand may overlap a little and on the other do not include unreported cases. Although the provision is of importance in the real estate field,[33] the restrictions appear to be so severe that the device is less used than the statute makers expected. Or perhaps the endless decision points make the device too clumsy to use. It is a remarkable series of complexities. From the administrative standpoint, without regard to the merits, it would have been an easier legal order if the return from the property of a collapsed corporation had either been left as a capital gain or made ordinary income.

Complexity

I have risked almost certain tedium in these illustrations because I have felt it imperative to demonstrate a vital technical point.

We are often told that the task of judicial administration becomes more difficult in contemporary times because problems become more complex. Partly, this simply means that they become bigger and thus more burdensome; a big industry has more documents in an antitrust case than a small one. But partly it means precisely what has been illustrated in the foregoing discussion. We have just looked at samples of new law made in four different fields in recent years, one chosen from rule-making, one from state uniform legislation, one from court decision and from promulgation by a body of experts, one from an act of Congress. The practical effect of all of the illustrations given is to add burdens to the judicial system. None of them creates new causes of action or new areas of the law; they simply revise existing bodies of law and add to their complexity. Each of the illustrations given adds dollar cost for the litigants and time cost for the courts. This is a good share of what we really mean when we say that the law is becoming ever more complex: we mean that we are multiplying decision points.

At the risk of being repetitive, let me say anew that every one of these additions to the judicial burden may be justified by considerations of justice, or of social welfare, or of the revenue, or whatever. Whether justified or not, they all add to the load on the elephant. Each comes under the leadership of the highest technical competence: the American legal system cannot do better than take the guidance of Professor Kaplan of Harvard (Procedure); Professor Llewellyn of Columbia and Chicago, and an immense supporting cast (Commercial Code); Professor Reese of Columbia (Conflicts); and the Internal Revenue Service and the staffs of the relevant Congressional committees (Collapsible Corporations). And yet—oh, cosmic impudence! I do not believe that each of these leaders is giving fully focused attention to the time-cost consequences of every change. This leads me to my summary *Recommendation* as to lawmaking:

13. Contrary to what I think is existing practice, every alteration of law ought to be seriously and scrupulously evaluated both in terms of its prime objectives and in terms of its litigation consequences. Complexities of marginal necessity should not be

added to any branch of the law where the operation will be time consuming or costly. The makers of substantive law should be, and often are not, consciously and sensitively alert to the problems of procedural law.

EASED ADMINISTRATION THROUGH RECONSTRUCTED SUBSTANCE

One possible solution of the court congestion problem is to exclude certain matters from the courts; the possibility of thus treating auto accidents has been discussed. A second possibility is to check the ever-increasing burden by reviewing current law changes, of whatever sort, to ensure that no avoidable new burdens are put on the legal system. A third possibility, to be discussed briefly here, is to review every area of the existing substantive law to see what changes might be made that would lighten the court load without cost to justice. In this section of this chapter are a few illustrations of such possibilities.

Domestic Relations

Promiscuity may be, and I think is, one of the great social evils of our time; but it is the marriages that, along with the automobiles, are crushing the legal system. As I said with some development of this point elsewhere, "One of the major misfortunes of contemporary America is the enormous number of grossly premature marriages based wholly on sexual attraction, resulting in prodigious numbers of divorces and the absence of family upbringing of children."[34] We have marriages by the million, with divorces in up to a third of them; and it is left to the courts to untangle the mess. In my own county, in many weeks the divorces may outnumber the marriages.

In these few paragraphs, let me take a narrow focus only on the problems of judicial administration created by divorce. Assume the all too frequent case: speedy acquaintance, speedy fornication, speedy marriage, speedy reproduction, and speedy repentance. Hypothetically, both parties were twenty when they met, and twenty-one when they had had enough.

Given those facts, we are brought back to the problem of miner James Kidd. We again face the question of just how much time, energy, and money the community is willing to spend in ameliorating the consequences of the young couple's improvidence. Let me start with the brutal assertion that although this problem needs to be handled somehow, the young couple does not have a God-given right to tie up the legal system of the United States. I suggest three areas of change in existing law.

Grounds. In my own jurisdiction, and in much of the rest of the United States as well, divorce, like marriage, has become consensual. That is to say, any couple may be married; and, equally, any couple may be divorced. If there is agreement between the parties, the plaintiff (almost always the wife by some strange relic of knightly chivalry) brings the action, alleging whatever grounds the particular jurisdiction happens to allow. The husband defaults, and judgment is given for the wife on a nominal showing.

When the system works this way, the court time taken is negligible. The usual ingredients of a divorce are first, the grounds; second, the custody of the children; and third, the financial arrangements. I have personally obtained divorces in two or three minutes of court time involving all of these elements, and I have no suggestion for any time-cost economies for the courts because none could be made in such cases. The couples come in as link sausages and come out as separate sausages; the procedure is as mechanical as that of a good packing house.

But in some of the cases, a very small number, there may be a dispute over grounds. My own limited but usual experience is that in more than half of the cases, by the time the parties see a lawyer, they are ready for a divorce; but in a substantial number, they are not. In these latter cases, only one party really wants a divorce. At that stage, there appears to be a possibility of a controversy over grounds. However, in almost every case, this evaporates in the course of settlement negotiations when the resisting party discovers that the pressing party really means it. Let me call this adjustment sector the interim period of the divorce.

Some small number of grounds cases actually last to the court room. My own experience here is very limited, but an expert who has handled some two hundred divorces in our jurisdiction tells me that approximately one hundred ninety were settled and disposed of by default; approximately ten were contested, and thus were the only ones to take any appreciable court time. Of those ten, there were grounds disputes in perhaps three. This kind of dispute in fact almost always comes to nothing—virtually invariably there are grounds enough to get the divorce. The time spent in disputing grounds is thus largely wasted, and although such time is not much at the end of the case, it is appreciable during the interim stage. A preliminary hearing is held to determine what the rights and duties of the parties shall be while the divorce is pending; because attitudes have not yet shifted, grounds testimony is frequently taken at this stage. The parties always hope that the presence or absence of grounds, or the quality of the grounds, will affect the judgment of the court on financial matters or on custody. The argument is that the other spouse is no good and therefore the asserting spouse should have either more money or less custody.

The suggestion has been made to me from a source that I deeply respect that grounds should be abolished altogether and that divorce, which is now as a practical matter consensual, should become so as a matter of law. My own knowledge is not sufficiently great to give me a personal opinion on this score, and therefore I can only make this *Recommendation:*

> 14. The grounds of divorce throughout the United States should be reconsidered to determine (a) whether their existence serves any socially useful purpose; and (b) whether controversies concerning them needlessly burden the administration of justice without serving any good end.

Economic Provisions. Divorce cases in which days and even weeks are consumed in determining how the economic interests of the couple shall be separated, whether by way of property distribution, alimony, or support, are all too common. To take a typical case, rising young executive *A* has been married to *B* for ten years. Let us assume that they married and have lived in a community property state, and that *B* had considerable separate property. The marriage has prospered financially but not personally, and at the end of ten years, *A* would rather be married to *X*, and *B* would rather be married to *Y*. The question presented from the standpoint of judicial administration is, how much time does the state have to give *A* and *B*—how long does it have to tie up a judge in a courtroom—to assist them to reshuffle their financial affairs so that they may make these new personal arrangements?

Here my suggestion becomes procedural rather than substantive, and so belongs in Chapter IV; but for the convenience of keeping the divorce matter in one place, let me take it up here. Sometimes the property distribution will be perfectly obvious: it may be simply a matter of looking at the cash in the bank, for example. But where many properties are involved, and where there are questions of what is community and what is not, and whether separate property has been commingled by its handling over the years, we should use a variation of the Massachusetts audit system. The divorcing couple, I submit, is entitled to an adversary proceedings only in some circumstances. I shall come back to the possible merging of inquisitorial as against adversary procedures in Chapter IV. Let me note here that in these cases we should appoint an accountant, at the expense of the parties, both to make an investigation and to make a report. Both parties should be required to answer questions, produce documents as they are desired, and cooperate. The accountant should be able to make his inquiries as would a businessman for the purpose of determining values. Businessmen constantly get workable values by telephone calls: they, "as reasonable men do in all affairs except the law courts, rely on hearsay."[35]

The parties on the receipt of the report, should be entitled to reject it, and have an adversary proceeding in court to review the same matters on the basis of judicial evidence, but this should be expressly conditioned upon having the losing side pay the costs of the proceedings, including fees of witnesses and counsel. I have seen a matter of this sort run for as much as five weeks of court time, and I submit that society simply does not owe this much of its attention to *A* and *B*.

Enforcement. The grounds cases are rare enough, and the big property disputes are also relatively unusual; the big loss of court time in domestic relations is in enforcement of the orders. In our own court of twenty-one divisions, I suspect that on a given day as many as ten judges may be giving some time to the problem of the spouse who was ordered to pay alimony or support for the children and has failed to do so.

These are likely to be the really grim problems, the hopeless cases. Typically, the couple probably did not have enough money to live as a family unit; this may well have contributed to the divorce in the first place. Certainly they do not have enough money to live as two families, with two roofs, two cars, two telephones, and all the rest. There is simply not enough money to go around. The result is a prodigious expenditure of time in trying to get blood out of turnips.

This is accentuated by the use of the contempt penalty. Putting the husband or father in jail probably will not add much to the family income. Yet there is no other device. The result is that in case after case, the court goes through motions, makes threats, gives warnings, and spins its wheels. I suggest:

First, that alimony be taken out of the system of enforcement by contempt, leaving the wife to the normal creditor's remedies of the jurisdiction. Let her garnish, execute, attach, whatever, with state laws amended to prevent discharge of employees because of garnishment. Let's get rid of contempt except where all other remedies have been exhausted and it appears that there is flagrant disregard of the duty to pay with complete capacity to do so.

Second, in the child support cases, I would make punishment automatic. Either the father pays or he doesn't. He may be unable to pay; he may have lost his job; he may have been ill. In that case, the burden has to fall somewhere. It will either fall on the wife to institute contempt proceedings, or it will fall on the husband to move for modification of the order. Because the burden must be on one or the other, I would put it on the husband to move for a modification, if he feels entitled to one.

Otherwise, the procedure should be automatic. All support payments should be made through the clerk of the court. When the payment does become late beyond the grace period, there should be an automatic warrant. The matter must then come through the probation office, with a recommendation, to a judge who can give a sentence. Hopefully, it may be slight; a day in jail frequently has the needed inspirational effect. But there is simply not the time or the money to give trials to all these contempts for the purpose of determining all of the circumstances. *Recommendation:*

15. Property distribution in substantial divorce cases should be the subject of an auditor's report, and court time should not normally be taken to determine these questions. The enforcement of divorce orders ought to be completely reconsidered, eliminating the contempt remedy for alimony violations and substituting other creditor's remedies. Failures to comply with child support orders should result in automatic penalties where the husband fails to obtain a modification of the order.

Probate

The present probate system in the United States has been widely criticized for its inherent delay and expense. With the exception of a few states where legislation authorizes administration of estates independent of court control, decedents' estates are administered under the control and supervision of the probate courts, with the judge participating at various stages of the process through judicial hearings on notice and issuance of court orders, even though there is no dispute among the persons interested.

Since 1962 the National Conference of Commissioners on Uniform State Laws and a subcommittee of the Real Property, Probate and Trust Law Section of the American Bar Association have been at work on the drafting of a complete code dealing with the estates of deceased and disabled persons and with certain transfers effective at death. A major purpose of the code is to simplify administration of estates and to return the judge to his rightful role as a decider of disputes. This will be accomplished by removing routine matters, about which there is no contest by the persons interested, from the judicial process. Such routine matters would be handled informally by an administrative officer of the court. Formal court proceedings, on notice and hearing, would be available at any stage if a dispute arose and court intervention were invoked by petition of any interested party. This plan will of course mean less judicial involvement, and a saving of time and expense for the court system.

In addition, the powers of the personal representative are expanded so that he need not turn to the court for judicial authorization in matters like sale or lease of realty, as he must at present in many states. He becomes in effect a trustee, not an officer of the court; his responsibility runs to the creditors and the heirs or devisees. Numerous other features of the code would reduce expense and eliminate court involvement. An illustration is the provision of the code for a self-proved will. This provision permits the testator and witnesses to acknowledge before a notary the due execution of the will; after the death of the testator it is unnecessary to prove execution—presently an expensive process when the witnesses are located in other states and depositions must be taken, even though no one is contesting the will.

Where the estate involves assets in several jurisdictions the code attempts to provide a unitary treatment of the estate and to reduce court proceedings in the other states.[36]

Commercial Law

Particularly in the field of creditors' rights, needed improvements are as much procedural as substantive. I shall therefore reserve most of these suggestions for the fourth chapter, but I here note a few:

(1) Every year in the United States an untold number of mortgages are foreclosed. This means as a practical matter that an action must be filed in court. It may mean that there is a hearing. In due course there will be an order. In my own jurisdiction, a typical case, even where there is a default, takes thirty-five days to get the judgment, thirty additional days for sale, and a six-month period of redemption.

The worst of it is that even in the default cases—indeed, particularly in the default cases where the property may have been abandoned—it is often necessary to have a receiver appointed. This means an application to the court, an appointment, and an eventual report. None of this business needs to be done in the courts at all, and in most cases, it should not be. Were the trust deed system used, the property would be placed in trust with a commercial institution. Upon failure of payment, after a reasonable grace period and all proper notices, title would simply pass.[37] Clearly there must be some protection against abuse, and such a system should allow the debtor to apply to a court for a stay in any appropriate case. But the existing system breeds litigation and dispute because in every instance the creditor is compelled to start a lawsuit. Were the burden transferred to the debtor, it may be safely assumed that the volume would reduce. *Recommendation:*

> 16. The legislatures generally should eliminate or markedly diminish or restrict the mortgage system. A trust deed system operating largely outside the courts should be substituted in its place, both for efficiency and economy.

(2) An unjustifiable burden on court time is the practice of allowing deficiency judgments in small consumer cases. Homeowner *H* buys a refrigerator on time. He fails to pay. Creditor *C* may repossess the refrigerator, sell it, buy it at the foreclosure sale for less than the amount owing, and then have a deficiency judgment against *H* for the difference. This is likely to be socially abusive and administratively burdensome. Moreover, with the expanded offering of defense services to poor persons, the amount of time spent wrangling to avoid deficiencies may reasonably be expected to increase.

There ought to be in this area one remedy or the other, but not both. *C* ought to be able to get a money judgment for the whole sum owing, if he wants it. Or he ought to be able to repossess by the normal possessory action of the jurisdiction. He ought not to be able to do both. A desirable remedial statute is Section 1812.5 of the *California Civil Code.*

(3) The entire matter of the existence of deficiency judgments even in substantial cases ought to be reconsidered. Professor Riesenfeld concluded a comprehensive article on *California Legislation Curbing Deficiency Judgments* with the observation, in effect, that the legislature has left too many decision points to the courts, decisions of policy matters that the courts have to determine on the basis of "elusive economic factors and preferences."[38]

(4) Insurance liquidation and receivership ought to become federal. Under existing law, it is common for a state insurance commissioner to apply in a state court for rehabilitation or liquidation of a state insurance company. There are strong factors in favor of keeping such a vital state matter in state hands altogether; but on the other hand, many of the state courts have no staff system for these purposes. A good-sized insurance company receivership may involve the bulk of a state judge's time for a protracted period. The going federal system of referees in bankruptcy and receivers, for all of its manifold and well-known imperfections, is at least more accustomed to these matters than the state courts.

The advantage in terms of uniform enforcement of claims and the ability to have ancillary proceedings in other federal courts is large. A relatively slight increase in the federal burden would materially reduce the state load. It would eliminate the proliferation out of one receivership of cases into other state courts all over the country. *Recommendation:*

17. A study should be made by state insurance com-

missioners or by the industry's attorneys through a
joint committee to determine the benefits and losses
in terms of speedier and easier judicial administration
if insurance liquidations and receiverships were transferred to the federal court system.

(5) Public construction bonds in many jurisdictions create
a frightful jumble of questions to be determined. A highway department may have one type of bond, a city another,
a school district a third. These have all simply grown in a
vast welter of confusion. There may be confusion as to when
a statute of limitations runs, or who can make a claim, or
what type of claim is covered by the particular type of bond.
A streamlined single bonding practice in the jurisdiction,
with attention given to achieving absolute clarity, so nearly
as this may be done, should materially reduce litigation.
This is no built-in panacea—the federal Miller Act, though
better than most state statutes, itself is an immense sponsor
of litigation that could be avoided by a clearer statutory spec-
ification of the nature of the claims covered. *Recommendation:*

> 18. Bonding laws on public works ought to be en-
> tirely reviewed. Priority disputes in particular should
> be eliminated by clear-cut lines as to rights, and small
> bonds, which are prolific litigation sponsors, ought to
> be eliminated entirely.

(6) Mechanic's lien statutes, for all their good social purpose, are an inheritance from a horse and buggy age. The
confusion they create, for example, as to when their time
begins to run and when the work is done gives rise to endless disputes. Many states have solved this problem by working out simple and clear recording devices. Even in a record

state, problems of priority exist in relation to mortgages. Much of this entire problem could be eliminated by a change in the substantive law to make the lending agency or the owner responsible for the disbursement of funds. This should not put an impossible burden on the lending agency—the supplier of materials should be required to give notice to the lender or owner, and there should be no burden on the owner to secure lien waivers from an uncounted number of unknown persons. *Recommendation:*

> 19. Mechanic's lien statutes, and all related legislation, should be reviewed and rewritten to achieve maximum clarity and simplicity.

CONCLUSION

The legal system of the United States simply cannot carry the weight that is on it. No matter what steps are taken, that weight will continue to grow. It will grow, first, because there will be more people, and prodigiously more. It will grow, second, because new problems will arise. Professor Maurice Rosenberg's lectures to the National College of State Trial Judges take up the consequences of expanding technology on the judicial work of the future. He assumes that by the year 2000, our present population of 200 million will have reached 300 million. The legal problems of an ever larger number of the aged will be with us. There will be the renovation rights cases, illustrated by the capacity of science to prolong life by the transplantation of the heart, for example. There will probably be a whole new body of law relating to students and their rights in relation to the schools and universities they attend.[39] There may be new

claims for employment rights; perhaps persons will be liti-
gating their right to be advanced in businesses and in law
offices as well as in trades under labor union contracts. There
will surely be an ever-larger body of cases involving intru-
sions on leisure, privacy, the joy of living. There will be
all the cases arising from inventions as yet unborn, from
skills as yet undeveloped.

Beyond all this, the courts perform a vital function as a
policy-making branch of government. Quite apart from the
pressure on the courts to accept routine commercial or other
purely private business is the pressure to accept public business. There is, particularly when the legislatures either of
states or of the nation are at dead center, pressure to accept
policy-making cases as a result of a widespread feeling that
courts are the best place to get policy made. On the national
level, segregation, redistricting, and church and state questions are turned into lawsuits for this purpose; locally, sharp
issues over zoning, regulation of business, community planning, and elections may similarly turn up in court. At times
the remote third branch of the government has been more
responsive to popular will and need than the executive or
the legislative. This function, too, must not be destroyed in
an engulfing tide of trivia.

Both to handle what we have and to make room for what
is coming, it is imperative that the law be cut down to a
size that the legal system can manage. We load ever more
burdens on the law, without adequately considering how
the law is to handle them. The units of the law are usually
treated as cases, but this is too simple; each case itself is a
bundle of decision points, or separate items around which
evidence, briefs, and argument may entwine themselves before decision. We need to do three things, and so my summary *Recommendation:*

20. (a) Vast areas of present legal work should be eliminated from the court system entirely; the automobile cases are the most likely candidate.

(b) Existing law should be expanded as needed, but always with a conscious judgment as to how the expansion will affect the operation of the court system that is to apply the new law.

(c) Existing substantive law should be reviewed to the end of seeking to make legal controversies not merely less frequent, but also smaller, by altering substantive law and eliminating from the individual cases as many decision points as we can.

IV

New Machinery for
the Law

The object of a court proceeding is to determine the truth. Guilty or not guilty; negligent or not negligent; more or less. We must therefore begin our consideration of the procedure for determining the truth with its most remarkable single feature: no one else pursuing the truth would proceed as do lawyers and judges. The law may or may not be a sure way of determining the truth, but it is surely the most awkward method ever devised.

The scientist, looking for a new and better formula for toothpaste, wishes to discover the truth. He begins by reading and evaluating what has been written; he may then talk to those who have some knowledge of the subject; and he will probably do some experiments on his own. He will not refuse to consider information because it is hearsay. If a friend tells him he learned something from a third person, the scientist may call the third person to verify the matter, or he may be content simply to rest on what has been told him. He is unlikely to appoint Mr. *A* to work up a "case" in favor of a particular method of achieving the ingredient he desires and Mr. *B* to work up a counter case, telling him all the reasons why Mr. *A*'s should not be tried. He will, in short, make an independent inquiry of his own, using all the sources that reasonable men use.

The same thing applies to the historian. He begins by reading the sources, goes on to interview anyone who may know anything about the subject first or second hand, looks for long gone documents and makes the best estimate he can as to their reliability. No historian seeks to find out what happened yesterday by appointing champions to develop various points of view among which he can choose.

The judge and the jury are more like the historian than the toothpaste researcher.[1] The historian may have the duty of finding out who won an election and why, and the court has the duty of finding out who hit the automobile and why. But the court traditionally proceeds by the adversary system: the judge becomes an umpire, and leaves it up to the two opposing counsel to develop the facts and law. The theory of the thing is that by the contending forces, and particularly by cross-examination, the judge or the jury will achieve the truth.

The fundamental illogic of the adversary system has its own series of justifications, some of them highly legitimate.[2] For example, anyone wishing to find out what happened at any point past, would, if he could, ask the people involved. The question may draw truth or falsehood, but the inquiry is an obvious starter. The law, particularly on the criminal side, cuts itself off from this obvious source of information; the accused is put under no obligation to respond to questions, and nothing can be made of it if he chooses not to do so. This departure from the historical or scientific method is well justified by the constitutional values of prevention of torture. Again, there is value in cross-examination, and the scientist and the historian might both learn more, if not faster, if they could compel persons to answer their questions by subpoena.

Nonetheless, the legal system gives to the adversary proceedings an overblown value. The opposing system of direct inquiry by the court is given a bad name, the inquisitorial system, to ensure its demise, and lawyers commonly place talismanic value on their traditional methods of inquiry.

I am advancing here no unconventional wisdom. The adversary system carried to its logical conclusion makes of the judge a little less than a baseball umpire, for the umpire has at least the authority to start the game on time on the appointed day. On the adversary theory, the opposing counsel have such final authority to represent their clients that it is no business of the judge even when the game starts. Counsel, unhappily, may be a long-winded, incompetent, contentious boob, and yet under the pure application of the adversary theory, the court has no function but to sit in place, rule on objections, and give instructions to the jury.

This umpire theory is today on the decline. There is now widespread belief that it is the duty of the judge to administer his courtroom and the cases in it as a part of his judicial duty; it is up to him to make the case march swiftly to a just conclusion.[3] The devices by which judges exercise their control, as well as the methods by which counsels plead, prepare, and present their cases, are rules or practices of procedure or evidence. This chapter will consider what changes in these procedures may be appropriate to speed judicial administration. These proposals, like those concerning substantive law, may reduce areas of decision or at least narrow decision points; they may on some occasions do this by increasing the authority or duty of the judge; or they may be simple mechanical suggestions for greater expedition.

A cautionary word is needed. As Justice Clark told the

Arden House Conference, "We do need to improve the procedures of the courts."[4] At the same time, changes, no matter how drastic, must not be the result solely of impatience; the goal of justice is ahead of the goal of expedition or economy. We could decide all the cases by throwing the files out the courthouse window and letting judgment depend on where they fall on the sidewalk. But we must hold in mind the principle of two observations by Mr. Justice Douglas:

> As calendar congestion increases, there are always those who would streamline procedure at the expense of basic rights. . . . Yet a man's rights will be greatly depreciated if he must wait two or more years to get inside a courtroom to establish them.[5]

Our task is to devise procedures that will expedite without infringing on basic rights.

MINOR MATTERS

Just as the ship that is in the water too long becomes encrusted with barnacles, so legal proceedings may become encrusted with tradition; and some of them may from time to time need to be scraped off. Some barnacles may not even be traditional—they may be fresh innovations and a costly waste of time.

Some judges require that counsel not leave his table, and that all exhibits be presented to a witness by a bailiff. In its most absurd and time-wasting form, counsel standing at his table takes a piece of paper from his briefcase; at a gesture, an aged and sluggish bailiff gets out of his chair, walks forward, takes the paper, carries it to the clerk's desk where it is marked, and then takes it to the witness. In the first place, all exhibits should have been marked in recess or before the trial started; in the second, if the lawyer is physically capable of doing so, he should trundle his own exhibit up to the witness and be done with it. Every time this minuet is danced, a minute or so is lost. It is, happily, a rare system.

A method that is a real abuse is the call of the calendar. In some jurisdictions, all counsel are notified to gather on a particular day while the judge calls out all of the cases on the docket. He inquires briefly as to the status of each and sets for trial those that are ready; or the call may be simply for the purpose of setting for trial. This is an aimless practice, and terribly expensive: when followed by a federal district judge in my own state, it has meant that a lawyer has had to come a distance of one hundred miles for the purpose of being present for two minutes. The particular lawyer would normally charge about $300 a day for his services and can sell all the time he has; if this expedition took him a total of five hours, the cost either to him or his client is around $200, and all to do something that could have been handled equally well by a postcard. If managed by a clerk, the judge could have been trying cases at the same time. We estimate that calendar calls under a recently instituted system in the state court costs either our office or our clients something like $1,500 a year.

There are other appearances for matters almost as clerical. In probate practice, it is the custom for the accounts of an estate to be settled by a "hearing," which is to say that there is a notice, and counsel actually goes to court with his papers. In the vast mass of probates, this appearance is completely aimless. Judge Jack G. Marks of the Superior Court of Pima County, Arizona, has sponsored a practice whereby these accounts are filed and noticed, but no one need appear unless the court asks for an appearance; as Judge Marks factually says, the previous practice was an "utter nonsensical waste of attorneys' time to accomplish acts which did not require the appearance of an attorney." If there is some necessity for an appearance, the matter could be rescheduled; but this almost never happens.

Other illustrations include the judges who will not let a lawyer hand them a document directly, but require that each item sent up to the bench come through the clerk or the bailiff; the practice of some judges of taking matters into chambers for leisurely discussion—there really ought to be a rule that every last bit of business should be done in the courtroom; or, in the most trifling and inconsequential instance of all, the practice of a former federal district judge in California of pausing for a moment of patriotic reverence in front of the American flag before he ascended his bench.

For a small example of the kind of economy that can be made with a little thought, it had been the practice of the appellate courts in my own jurisdiction not to set the order of cases in advance, but rather to require all lawyers to appear in the courtroom on the morning of the day in which the case was to be heard. The schedule would then be set in open court. In a typical instance, this meant that at least six lawyers made a completely unnecessary trip to the court, with the resultant waste of either having to return to their offices or standing by. A more recent practice of the appellate courts sets a schedule in advance. The economies are real.

Still another traditional practice that is by no means invariably wise is the practice of calling witnesses one at a time, one after the other. The alternative is the so-called conference method of trial. There are occasions, particularly when the tensions between the sides are not great, in which it may be more profitable to take several witnesses at once.

In a default divorce, for example, if the jurisdiction requires
the testimony of the complaining party and a witness, the
two can be sworn together and can be briefly interrogated
consecutively with both standing in front of the bench. But
also in contested litigation, it may be faster and more efficient to put several sworn witnesses around the table at the
same time.

I have tried the system both in the courtroom and on
depositions, and have found it an immense time-saver. For
example, if a witness who is testifying generally about land
use can testify together with an engineer who completely
understands the maps involved, movement back and forth
between the two makes for more sensible and faster testimony than getting places from one and practices from the
other. In big commercial cases, with substantial foundation
problems, this method is particularly useful; the witness in
charge of production, the witness who keeps the files, and
the witness who sends the bills can most conveniently be
taken as a group. Very frequently the businessman and his
bookkeeper would best be examined together.

Every judge, governing procedures in his own courtroom,
should be conscious of the cost of proliferating decision
points. For illustration, in 1967 I tried a case of great public
concern in a state other than Arizona. That state has not
adopted the Canons of Ethics of the American Bar Association, and had never conclusively determined whether court
proceedings could be televised. A local station applied for
the privilege.

The trial judge, exceptionally experienced, was troubled
with what was a nearly new question in his jurisdiction. He
thereupon first took testimony on the details of television
procedures and then directed full-scale briefs and arguments.
My own position and that of my client is one of almost apo-

plectic opposition to courtroom television or broadcasting, and we comprehensively briefed and argued the issue involved. The combined cost in travel and in counsel time on this issue was around $1,500.

The judge eventually decided that there should be no television, making clear that if he had not felt compelled by the legal authorities, he would have permitted it on a case-by-case basis, determining the relevant factors in each instance. Had he not felt himself confined by the authorities, the solution that tempted him would have been, administratively, the worst possible alternative. A court may televise or not televise; I would hope the latter. But either alternative would at least avoid the consumption of time spent in deciding what to do. If the issue can be raised in every case, the procedure will again put a lawsuit in front of a lawsuit.

A substantial number of judges are time oriented; the number is a minority of those whom I have seen, but it is still substantial. But almost none is cost oriented. Most judges are salaried, and are not thinking at all in terms of the hourly charges of the counsel before them. Judicial training programs ought to drill and drill and drill into the minds of the judges, so that they never forget it, that the time clock is running. If counsel on both sides are charging $30 an hour, then the judge who tolerates an avoidable minute of court time has just taxed the litigants one dollar, and this as surely as if the tax were enacted by the state legislature. Every requirement and every procedure ought to be evaluated in every instance on a time-cost basis. This leads me to these *Recommendations:*

21. Statewide and local judges' conferences should go over the minutiae of their own procedures to sat-

isfy themselves inch by inch and step by step that they
are operating as economically as they can, both in
time and in overall costs to lawyers and clients as well
as to taxpayers. It will be a rare judge who will not
find at least one thing he can do more efficiently if
there is a tight re-examination of every separate activity.[6]

22.   Procedure should be altered to permit conference-type trials or part trials in appropriate cases.

COST CONTROL OF LITIGATION

The costs of bread and milk, of suits and shoes, of houses
and cars go up, but a man can still buy himself a good lawsuit for $15. Counsel fees rise, so that retainers increase,
but if a plaintiff is able to find an attorney who will take
his case on a percentage basis, all he needs to start his case
is a filing fee. The entire process of which the case is a part
is not of immense cost to the taxpayers; a good moon rocket
or a naval vessel costs more. Nonetheless, as was noted
earlier, the operation of the legal system of the State of
New York costs its taxpayers approximately $120 million a
year. Under our system, the parties use this $120 million
system essentially free, so far as the state is concerned; the
contributions in jury fees or filing fees leave a heavy portion
of the cost to be borne by the taxpayers.

For this reason, it does not matter whether a party wins
or loses. To take an extreme case, I once defended a civil
treble damage antitrust matter in which the complaint was
so unfounded that the plaintiff did not even appear in court
when the case was submitted to the jury; but the defendants paid the better part of $20,000 in costs and fees all the
same, with no recompense at all.

The English use a different system. Under their practice, the losing party must pay the costs of the winning party, and these costs include the attorneys' fees.[7] Students have concluded that the English cost system does in a substantial and material way contribute to the fact that English dockets are much less burdened than our own. There is an oft-asked question as to whether it is desirable to control the volume of our own litigation by raising its price. Such a proposal is usually developed from the English practice, not as a device for reducing further costs for the benefit of the state, but as a device for charging the attorneys' fees of the winning party against the loser. Although there have been specialized statutes for this purpose in particular areas, there has been no general legislation in the United States of this kind outside of Hawaii.[8]

Whatever the virtues of the system for the English, it goes terribly against the grain for Americans. The high cost of legal services that must be paid under the existing system is distressing in a society that really does not want people to be denied justice because they are not rich enough to pay for it. In the absence of comprehensive studies, I am not sufficiently persuaded by the English system to wish to spend time talking about it.

But short of the English system, there are some very constructive steps to be considered. If cost allocation can be used as a device to reduce court congestion without thereby pricing justice out of the market, then it may be highly desirable. Hence, it has been suggested that unreasonable conduct in lawsuits or unjustifiable litigation might be controlled by imposing substantial costs.[9]

The existing rules contain major devices for this purpose. Rule 36 on admissions permits one side to ask the other to admit certain matters. If the other side refuses to admit, then the asking side must put on its proof in court, thus both taking court time and running up the costs for the preventing party; but if it appears that the refusal to admit was unreasonable, those costs, including attorneys' fees, can be charged against the party that refused to admit. Also relevant is Rule 68 of the Rules of Civil Procedure relating to offer of judgment. Under this rule, the defendant may in appropriate circumstances offer to let the plaintiff take a judgment for a specified amount of money. If the plaintiff declines and later recovers less than the amount of the offer, the plaintiff must pay the costs incurred after the offer has been made.

Rule 36 has been used a little, but not nearly as much as it could be;[10] partly this has been because of ambiguities in its terms. The rule is currently being strengthened by a proposal of the Advisory Committee on Civil Procedure, a proposal submitted to the bar of the country for comment and consideration at about the same time as these lectures are given. This seems to me a highly desirable procedure. Carried to its logical conclusion, the admissions practice could put the whole burden of trial on the losing party by permitting the parties to call for admissions on every single issue in the case, the cost of proving any of them to be charged to the loser. I would modify this to permit such charges under the admissions rule wherever, in the reasonable discretion of the court, the issue was clear. I would also have every issue and every fact automatically subject to a demand for admission at the pretrial conference, this procedure to be utilized as I shall discuss in connection with pretrial. This leads to the following *Recommendation:*

    23. Rule 36 of the Rules of Civil Procedure, the admissions rule, should as a matter of standard prac-

tice be used in every case to put the cost of proof, including counsel fees, on the losing party wherever the issue is unreasonably disputed.

A variation of the offer of settlement device is the Gumpert Plan, so named for its author, Judge Emil Gumpert of the Los Angeles Superior Court. Judge Gumpert, who is highly regarded in California for his effectiveness in disposing of auto accident cases, has proposed a plan for such cases in which the parties are required to negotiate in good faith for a settlement. The plaintiff is required to make a demand and the defendant is required to make an offer or state that he will pay nothing. The demand and the response are to be sealed and filed. When the case is done, the court opens the file and has discretion to allow or not to allow costs, interest on the judgment from any point subsequent to the accident, and attorneys' fees and expert witness fees to whichever party ought to get these benefits. For the purpose of determining these allocations, the court is to take into account the demand and offer as well as other relevant circumstances.

The Gumpert Plan failed passage in the California Legislature at the 1965–66 session, but clearly warrants further consideration.[11] Judge Gumpert has observed that "although this measure failed passage, I am confident that some such legislation will have to be adopted if we are to retain with the court structure the disposition of personal injury litigation."[12]

It is imperative that some form of the Gumpert Plan, whether as legislation or as a revision of Rule 68, should be adopted. The proposal is so important that I pause a little with technical detail. The present Rule 68 provides only for an offer of judgment; in other words, it gives an alternative only to the defendant. This is wrong. The system ought to work both ways. The only way to keep cases from getting to trial once they are filed (apart from abandonment) is to settle, and all settlement devices ought to be used. Other possibilities in this direction are to be discussed. It is reasonable, as a condition of the use of the judicial system, that society require litigants to use every effort to agree. For this purpose, society may reasonably put a very substantial premium on settling by creating a substantial penalty against not settling. Rule 68 can provide this device.

Therefore, in any case in which one side wants the other side's money, the plaintiff ought to be required, after discovery is over and when he knows as much about the case as he is going to know, to make a meditated demand; and similarly, the defendant ought to be required to make a meditated offer. The best way to obtain this quality of meditation is to make it expensive to use the demand and offer for purely tactical purposes. If in a $10,000 auto accident case, the demand is $12,000 and the offer is $8,000, and if one side or the other is going to be stuck with an additional $2,500 of charges depending upon whether the jury comes in high or low, there will be a premium on settlement. This is the kind of simple revision that is wholly within the power of the rulemakers, and that can be handled by the adjustment of Rule 68. It seems to me of high importance that this be done, and I stress the observation of Judge Gumpert that something of the kind is imperative if auto accident litigation is not to be moved out of the courts entirely. This leads me to the following *Recommendation:*

> 24. Rule 68 of the Rules of Civil Procedure should
> be revised to establish a system of demand by the

claimant and offer by the defendant. Costs, including counsel fees, should be charged if the eventual determination of the case shows either that the demand was too high or the offer too low.

STIPULATIONS AND SETTLEMENTS

No concept of the adversary system is endurable under which the parties can, in their own discretion, save what they have for proof in court. The procedure now diminishes the value of surprise as an instrument of justice; as I once developed in another place, Abraham Lincoln might never have gotten Hannah Armstrong's boy off in the famous *Almanac* case if contemporary discovery practices had existed and had eliminated the surprise as to where the moon was on the night in question.[13] But we simply have neither the courtrooms, nor the judges, nor the time, to permit these time bombs to blow off regularly in the courthouse; in the preceding section, and in this one and in the next, I discuss devices for either derailing the cases before they get to trial or expediting them after they arrive, and all these devices are at the cost of surprise.

Tax Court Stipulations

The stipulation procedures of the Tax Court of the United States present intriguing possibilities for trial courts generally. Rule 31(b) of the Tax Court Rules of Practice requires stipulations of the parties on "all material facts that are not or fairly should not be in dispute." All entries or summaries from books of account and other records, documents and other evidence are to be the subject of conference between counsel, "and both shall endeavor to stipulate all facts not already stipulated." If the parties are unable to agree, they may submit their own proposed stipulations and the court may simply adopt them by court order.[14]

As a substantial consequence of its stipulation procedure, the Tax Court is marvelously current on its docket. As of the date of these lectures, it has pending tax claims in the amount of $1.3 billion. In a given year, six to seven thousand cases are filed. Large numbers of the cases are settled; the rest are disposed of by a bench of sixteen judges, which keeps the docket current. The heavy output judges of that court write forty to fifty opinions a year.

The consequence of the Tax Court rule on courtroom time is that cases frequently require only an hour or so of evidence; an abnormally big case might run three or four days. In December, 1967, one judge anticipated hearing seven cases in El Paso, Texas, in four hours. In another case, the parties had asked for two weeks and had subpoenaed fifty-six witnesses. The Tax Court judge, rigorously pressing the use of the stipulation practice, heard the matter in nine court hours with six witnesses. In the spring term, 1967, the Tax Court handled 121 trials in 32 cities in 446 actual hours for an average time of roughly $3\frac{2}{3}$ hours. These are fairly representative of the trial sessions of that court.[15]

Three substantial Tax Court stipulations, furnished by the Clerk of the Tax Court as examples of stipulations that materially shorten trial time, averaged about twenty-three typed pages.[16] They contained agreements as to documents; financial records of various payments, agreed to the decimal point; corporate histories; records of loans; records of purchases; and much other information. They represent, in short, exactly the kind of information that competent trial counsel ought to be able to agree on in any civil case.

This system is obviously not completely transferable to

the trial courts. The Tax Court matters are partially pre-digested by the Internal Revenue Service and there is no equivalent in general civil litigation. Moreover, Tax Court judges with whom I have discussed the device report that they have special controls. If the taxpayer is stingy in his stipulations, his case can go off the docket and wait. If government counsel is unreasonable, the tax judge can report the matter somewhat unpleasantly to his superiors. Moreover, the constitutional right to jury trial is not involved. There are likely to be more objectively determinable facts in a tax case (how many dollars were spent for a particular purpose?) than in a negligence case (how fast were the respective cars going?). Hence, the stipulation procedure is no panacea. Nonetheless, something of the sort could be much more used than it is in civil cases generally, with immense benefit to the docket. This leads to another *Recommendation:*

> 25. Close study should be given to the revision and enforcement of existing rules relating to pretrial conferences so as to increase the number of factual stipulations after the fashion of the Tax Court practice.

Mediation

One other special federal device that might well be put to use to reduce court congestion parallels the federal mediation and conciliation service in labor disputes. This suggestion is wholly experimental, and I therefore offer it diffidently. Under this proposal, after discovery is complete but before the pretrial conference, a mediation division of the clerk of court's office would attempt by direct negotiation to bring the parties to settlement. This procedure is not merely entirely out of court, it is also out of the judiciary; it would take no judicial time at all. The mediators in the auto accident field, for example, would certainly not be judges and also need not be lawyers; they might better be experienced claims adjusters. Such personnel might well be far more able than many judges to size up the case and recommend solutions.

Of course a routine lawsuit is not like a routine labor dispute, which may readily lend itself to mediation; most lawsuits are narrower in the number of issues and in the matters to be decided than even small labor disputes. The analogy is perhaps closer to the conciliation services at work in some courts in the domestic relations field. In those courts, nonjudicial personnel are in fact able to deal with the parties in a semiprofessional way, and there is some good in it.

The system could work badly. It may be too difficult within a civil service pay structure to find qualified personnel to manage it. It may be that the whole procedure might become simply another blind alley and further delay the litigation process. As one sees good ideas tried and fail, caution sets in. But the proposal does seem worth a try, and I therefore make this *Recommendation:*

> 26.   An experiment should be undertaken to mediate money demand cases, using only nonjudicial personnel. The most obvious possibility is to have trained insurance adjusters representative of the court consult with both sides in auto accident cases to try to lead the parties to agreement.

Settlement Conferences

In the federal system, only about 12 per cent of the cases are actually tried;[17] if this could be reduced to 10 per cent, the relief would be tremendous.

The final device for getting the case off the calendar is to settle it on the eve of trial. A likely possibility is at the pretrial conference. Here the settlement discussion may be led by the judge, either the one who is to try the case or another. The conference itself may be either the regular pretrial conference or may be a special settlement conference.

In 1963 California instituted a separate special settlement conference.[18] The system depends on attorney preparation and good faith participation; these and many other major procedural details are covered in the Van Alstyne and Grossman work cited in the note.

I have heard glorious accounts of the success of the settlement procedures, particularly during 1965 and 1966. Van Alstyne and Grossman give figures of 91 per cent settlements in one group of 214 cases and 95 per cent settlements in another group of 266 cases, with estimated savings of 900 trial days.

The present California practice provides either for a special pretrial settlement conference if requested by either party, or a voluntary joint request where settlement seems highly likely but has not quite been reached. Weekly figures for late August and early September, 1967, were 34 per cent, 22 per cent, and 15 per cent settlements in the special pretrials, and 42 per cent, 53 per cent, and 60 per cent in the jointly requested pretrials. The relatively low percentage in the special cases is said to be partly the product of a general weakening of California pretrial as a result of a modification of the whole requirement; my report is that some counsel are now miserably prepared for special settlement conferences. Clearly, the core of the system is having a judge who, by virtue of his own experience, knows what a case is worth. One particularly expert Los Angeles trial judge reports that he is settling about 175 cases a year. Others are less successful.

Under the California system, whenever possible the settlement judge is not the trial judge. The theory here is that candor cannot be achieved if a side confesses weakness before a judge who is going to try the case; before the trial judge, counsel is almost compelled to take a stronger position than in fact he believes he can hold. Because the judge at the pretrial conference usually should be the judge who will try the case, the California system can result in two pretrials, one for general purposes and the other for settlement.

The strongest statement I have seen in behalf of having the same judge handle the settlement conference and the trial comes to me from one of the most experienced and most effective federal judges. He says:

> Where the pre-trial judge is the same judge who tries the case, pre-trials can be an effective instrument not only in saving trial time, but also, and more important, in disposing of the case without trial. A competent pre-trial judge requires both sides to disgorge all of their evidence, including of course the medical reports. Thus at pre-trial both sides and the judge should know everything there is to know about the case. Competent lawyers and a competent judge, armed with this knowledge, and based on their experience in the trial of similar cases, know what the case is worth on settlement. Consequently, the pre-trial judge should require both sides to discuss in detail the prior settlement negotiations, including the last offer from each. He should then recommend a settlement figure.
>
> If the pre-trial judge has the confidence of his bar, the lawyers for both sides welcome the judge's recommendation. It takes at least part of the responsibility

off their shoulders. They can go back to their clients and say, "We think this, but the experienced and fair judge who is going to try the case thinks this." After this presentation the plaintiff's lawyer has no trouble whatever with his client, and the defendant, usually really an insurance company, gets the message.

Even where the case is not settled at pre-trial, serious settlement negotiations have begun, and two or three days before the trial the good pre-trial judge who is also the trial judge calls in the lawyers again for an up-to-date pre-trial and settlement conference. Even if the case does not settle after the second conference, much trial time is saved by the trial judge being prepared to try that particular case based on his prior knowledge of it and on the complete disclosure which has been made by both sides under the eye of the court.

As one who has very little direct auto accident experience, I must again be diffident in my conclusions, but for me the views just expressed are persuasive. There is far too much mystery, deviousness, and want of candor about settlements. Lawyers maneuver to make the subject of settlement "come up" as if there were some indelicacy in facing the problem frontally. In almost every case, either side can lose something; settlement discussions ought always to be direct and forthright. Lawyers cannot sensibly appraise a case without knowing all about it, and because there is supposed to be complete disclosure at pretrial, there should not after that point be any secrets to be kept from the judge. The real fear if the settlement judge tries the case is that if the judge's recommendation is not followed, he may somehow take it out on the party who disagrees with him. This is a real and legitimate fear; I have on occasion been simply badgered by a judge, sometimes to the point of yielding to a position against my better judgment. There are badgering judges and there are judges who are anxious to run away from the responsibility of decision by forcing settlement; but in my experience, such judges are, independently, so poor that this abuse does not make them much worse. On balance, I conclude with this *Recommendation:*

> 27. In every case that admits of settlement, there should be a pretrial conference that has settlement as one of its prime aims. At such a conference all parties should be required, with the penalty of not being able to use any other information at the trial, to disclose every fact bearing on settlement. The court should then recommend a settlement figure and lead the discussion. The conference may best be held with the judge who will try the case, though this is not imperative. Rule 16 of the Rules of Civil Procedure should be amended accordingly.

SUMMARY JUDGMENT AND ITS RELATION TO PRETRIAL

Of all of the conventional procedural devices, summary judgment is the one best calculated to reduce court dockets. The failure to make greater use of this remedy is an unhappy monument to the law's resistance to change. The vanguard position for making the most of summary judgment was taken by the late Judge Charles E. Clark, the draftsman of the rules that include the remedy. In these observations, I want to align myself with Judge Clark's position; but I would also make concrete suggestions to push the use of the remedy beyond the point to which he was ready to go.

A good illustrative starting point for conflicting views is *California Apparel Creators v. Wieder of California*.[19] This was a suit by persons in the garment business in California seeking to bar persons in the same business in New York from using the word "California" or some variant of it as a brand name. The theory was that clothes made in California are superior to clothes made elsewhere, and that the inferior quality of the defendants' goods would injure the reputation of plaintiff's goods. The defendants moved for summary judgment, which was granted. Judge Clark, affirming for the majority of the Court of Appeals, noted that although affidavits were offered stating the conclusion that California clothes are better than New York clothes, no actual evidence of any kind was pointed to, nor was there any showing of definite standards of quality. There was, in short, no way shown by which the allegation could be proved, and no evidence to support any plausible theory. Hence, the majority said, "The grant of the summary judgment was therefore appropriate."

Judge Learned Hand dissented, criticizing the use of summary judgment. He said:

> When I see, as I am constantly seeing more and more, the increasing disposition to make use of that remedy, I cannot help wondering whether there is not danger that it may not rather impede, than advance, the administration of justice. It is an easy way for a court with crowded dockets to dispose of them, and the habit of recourse to it readily becomes a denial of that thorough, though dilatory, examination of the facts on which justice depends even more than upon a studious examination of the law; for a mistake of law can always be reviewed.[20]

Alas, there is far too little basis for Judge Hand's concern. Rule 56 of the Federal Rules of Civil Procedure provides that a court, on consideration of the pleadings, depositions, answers to interrogatories, admissions, and affidavits, may give judgment for either party without going to trial at all if it finds that "there is no genuine issue as to any material fact and that the moving party is entitled to a judgment as a matter of law." In other words, after the case is prepared and before it is tried, the court may look at all of the preparatory materials and may decide that there is nothing to try, that on the basis of the facts as shown in those papers, in the light of the law, one side or the other should win. In that case, the judge may wind the matter up then and there, without ever having a trial. The practice is developed from the English method of disposing of cases of no merit; it has been expanded in American law, particularly in the twentieth century, and received its maximum present statement in the Federal Rule just stated.[21]

Summary judgment procedure is a method for determining whether there is a "genuine issue," and whether that genuine issue is as to a "material fact." If a judge can, in an hour or two, determine on the basis of what is before him that a trial would be aimless, then there is no point in spending several days in trying the case.

Nonetheless, the rule is applied in stingy fashion. It is often said that the summary judgment may not be used when there is the "slightest doubt" as to the facts, and all too often courts are unwilling to use the remedy if facts might at some later time turn up that might sustain an otherwise defective case.[22] As Judge Clark has said,

> If this is to be applied as it is stated, there can hardly be a summary judgment ever, for at least a slight doubt

can be developed as to practically all things human.
. . . This natural consequence is not merely the elimination of a useful remedy for effective disposition in
many cases; it also presents a serious question of policy as to the forcing of litigants to a long trial on
clearly worthless claims.[23]

Accepting Judge Clark's view, let me see whether I can
advance the ball a little by the following observations.

Every case at the appropriate point ought to be subject
to a motion for summary judgment. In the current practice,
there are three principal methods of bringing before a court
the question of whether a case should be tried at all. The
first of these is the motion to dismiss the complaint for failure to state a claim on which relief can be granted. I am
tempted to advocate the abolition of this classical motion as
a plain waste of time. Very few cases are conclusively disposed of at this point; the dismissal, if granted, is almost
always with leave to amend. The procedure thus becomes
essentially dilatory; as a matter of personal practice, I have
scarcely made such a motion in years and would do so only
if there were clearly no jurisdiction in the court in which
the matter was pending.[24]

The second motion is for judgment on the pleadings. The
complaint is in, the answer is in, and either party can then
contend that on the basis of the issues as framed, he should
prevail. This is clearly a useful motion, which may render
expensive discovery unnecessary; but its use is limited to
those cases in which, even if facts were established, the result
would be unaffected.

Finally comes the motion for summary judgment, in which
the court may search the entire discovery record. The judge
may not consider merely the issues that were presented in

the motion for judgment on the pleadings, but also everything else that has been developed in the case.

In my view, every case should come up for consideration
of summary judgment at the pretrial conference, arising at
the court's own instance if the parties have not raised the
question before.[25] At this point, the counsel should be required to specify what they regard as the issues of the case,
and the court should stabilize the issues in the pretrial order.
In this connection, the court should require both sides to
show, whether from the pleadings, or from the discovery
documents, or from affidavits by persons having direct knowledge of the matter, that there is some evidence to go into the
record in respect to the particular issue. On any issue on
which facts cannot be shown, there should be summary
judgment.

The great, unutilized portion of Rule 56 that could really
reduce trial time is the provision for partial summary judgment—a party may move in the case "for a summary judgment in his favor upon all *or any part thereof.*" The "any
part" provision is relatively rarely used, so that most courts
give judgment either on the whole case or on none of it; for
the purpose of cutting costs and saving trial time, they should
commonly give judgment on part.

This much can be done even in the negligence cases, and
this without any treason to the doctrine that the place to
determine disputed facts is a trial. In the normal negligence
case, there will usually be some conflicting evidence as to
negligence. Concretely, the plaintiff says that the defendant
was driving too fast and defendant says he was not. This
issue cannot be determined on summary judgment—it is a
question of fact as to which there is a genuine issue, and it
is clearly material. But in the same case, the defendant may

have raised an issue of contributory negligence on which he has no evidence at all; the issue was put into the defense simply because defense counsel, quite properly, always includes a contributory negligence defense in the hope that something will turn up on discovery. But in this case, nothing did. By the time the case reaches pretrial, such optimism should be too late. The court ought to ask the defendant to show at least some evidence that is going to be offered at trial to support the contributory negligence defense, and if nothing is forthcoming, the court ought to grant partial summary judgment then and there on that issue. So, also, with questions of proximate cause and assumption of risk.

In other words, if summary judgment cannot be used to dispose of the whole case, it ought to be used to eliminate as many decision points as possible. Summary judgment, instead of being the exception, should be the rule on at least some issues.

To permit more effective use of summary judgment, rule changes are needed. As the law presently stands, a motion for summary judgment requires a ten-day notice; there is no express provision that the judge at the pretrial conference can rule on the various issues from this standpoint unless the trigger had earlier been pulled by this notification. Hence, in some instances, cautious counsel put in motions for summary judgment on every possible issue before the pretrial conference. This is needlessly elaborate. The rules should be changed so as to provide that every issue in the case is subject to summary judgment at the pretrial, without any advance procedure. It should be understood and anticipated that at this stage the judge will narrow the case as much as he possibly can. To make this procedure effective, Rule 36 on admissions must also be considered. It should be understood that, as to every fact or legal question in the case, either side may be subject to a demand for admission at the pretrial conference, either by opposing counsel or by the court. This is for two distinctly separate purposes. First, counsel may here be required to admit the validity of documents or their copies when there is no reasonable ground to doubt their validity, simply to save expense and bother; second, counsel should be subject to a demand to admit the facts that may bear on the application for summary judgment. In the *California–New York Clothes* case, for example, either side might be called upon to admit marketing facts that in reason ought to be known to all and that, if admitted, would permit summary judgment. If such facts are then denied, the adverse party may at least be put to the expense his opponent incurs in proving them.

These thoughts lead me to this *Recommendation:*

> 28. At the pretrial conference, the judge should think of the case as a series of decision points or issues, the disposition of each of which will take courtroom time. It should be his goal at this point to strip the case of as many decision points as can possibly be removed. He may be able to decide the whole case by summary judgment, and in so doing he should insist that the parties offer then and there whatever of substance they expect to have at trial that will show that there is a material fact worth trying. Applying this standard, if he cannot dispose of all of the issues of the case, he should then decide as many as he can to the end of reducing the scope of the trial as much as possible. He can preserve absolutely the right to try genuine issues of material fact without thereby suffering the trial of any nongenuine issues of immaterial fact.

CREDITORS' CASES AND
COMMERCIAL LITIGATION

Commercial cases involving accountants or voluminous books and records can be either endless consumers of court time or short and snappy. Speed is almost always a possibility, particularly if procedures are somewhat changed. Most can be accelerated by stipulation, and the court's first duty here is to press for a Tax-Court-style stipulation. In a recent matter involving hundreds of thousands of dollars, which was expected to take some weeks to try, each side designated accountants to answer precise questions. The joint answers of the accountants then went into evidence as a stipulation. Trial time was cut to a few days and costs were greatly reduced. Other suggestions follow.

There is no inherent virtue in referring matters to masters. If the master is himself qualified only as the judge is qualified, and if he proceeds in the same way, then the procedure has merely established another judge and another courtroom, without serving any larger purpose. But if the master can have a qualification that the judge does not have, and if he can follow procedures that the judge does not use, then there may be great virtue in the master.

This device is particularly serviceable in detailed questions of accounts. In such cases, auditors or accountants ought to be used. In a recent case in our own office, for example, twenty-four mortgages were being foreclosed with six lien claimants. Bigger cities and bigger enterprises will have transactions infinitely more complex. In these cases, the courts ought to be free to go straight to the inquisitorial system, for all its horrid name. The courts should be authorized to designate an accountant to look into the matter, to get the facts, to make a report. The accountant should be free to examine books, records, and papers, and these should have to be produced, with penalties for failure to do so. The accountant should receive information from all of the parties, of course, and where proper, he may hear arguments; but basically, he should be called upon to do an independent accountant job. Life is simply too short to permit the proving of complex accounts, a paper at a time, with all the limitations of the hearsay rule.

If the parties are dissatisfied with the report of the accountant, they should of course be entitled to challenge it. I do not propose that a day in an accountant's office be substituted for a day in court. But if the accountant chosen were an independent expert, there would normally be no challenge to most of his conclusions, and all that would remain to be determined would be their legal consequences. This result can be encouraged by requiring the challenging party to pay the costs of the other side if the challenge is not well warranted.

This leads to the following *Recommendation:*

> 29. Courts should seek to avoid hearing accounting cases a document at a time. In such matters, independent expert accountants should be appointed by the courts to make reports, and they should be entitled to proceed in the normal manner of accountants rather than by the procedures of court proof. Only the exceptions to their reports should require court procedues.

The poor litigant staggers through all of the procedures of the law. He retains his counsel, sees his complaint filed, waits his eternity for a trial, goes through discovery, has the

trial, and finally wins. He has a judgment. Now what can he
do with it?

The procedures for enforcing judgments are located deep
in one of the worst morasses of the law. Perhaps he can execute the judgment. This, if he looks at a standard legal
encyclopedia to find out what he is doing, will mean that he
obtains "a judicial writ issuing from the court where the
judgment is rendered, directed to an officer thereof, and running against the body or goods of a party, by which the
judgment of the court is enforced."[26] As a practical matter,
this means that he can have the sheriff take the property of
the person against whom he has a judgment. But he must
proceed cautiously, or he will find himself starting in again
on a whole new lawsuit, for if he continues to turn the pages
of that same encyclopedia, he will discover that there are
777 pages in that volume on the law of executions; the mind
boggles at the number of cases of litigation over executions,
but it is a great many thousands in this one source alone. If
the claimant is concerned that the property may disappear
during the long course of litigation, he may attach it, and
this may be a remedy after judgment as well; or if he wishes
to cut off funds flowing to his debtor before they reach their
destination, he may sue out a writ of garnishment. A leading
work on the relations of debtors and creditors has some fifty
index entries on attachment and has separate discussions on
garnishments in relation to bills of lading, community property, corporate stock, liability insurance, negotiable interests,
and numerous other subjects.[27] The borders of these remedies
are frequently hazy. For example, under much existing law
if real property is held in trust, and produces income, one
may seek garnishment against the income, but not against
the trust; similarly, one cannot attach the trust, because for
reasons of no contemporary relevance at all, the trust is an

equitable interest and attachment is a legal remedy. Hence, there must be a creditor's bill to reach the equitable assets. All of this is costly foolishness.

Not merely for justice to the parties involved, but to reduce the load on the courts, I make this *Recommendation:*

> 30. There should be one method of enforcing judgments and the distinctions as to the form of the process ought to be abolished. The process should reach assets of whatever nature, unless exempt, and regardless of who may hold the assets. There should be an elimination of all technical distinctions between garnishment, attachment, execution, creditor's bill, and similar devices. The process for enforcing judgments should be continuing in nature; the practice of successive garnishment of income by separate legal proceedings at regular intervals should be eliminated, and the garnishment should stand good until it is terminated by some appropriate order or by payment. There should be interstate enforcement of process. In the federal courts, one can in a simple way enforce in one state a judgment taken in another. A similar arrangement should exist for the enforcement of judgments between sister states.

It is in the relatively small claims cases that the law's delay is most commonly used as a shield; even in large claims cases, this is easy enough. Any lawyer can tie up a claim for a long time—perhaps for years—by the standard dilatory defenses. If the claim is for, say, $2,000, which the plaintiff says he loaned to the defendant, and if the defendant simply denies the loan, or claims that he was defrauded by false promises and assurances into borrowing the money in the first place, or counterclaims for something or other, he will raise thereby a genuine issue of material fact. The defense might evaporate with discovery, but the amount involved is so small that there will be some reluctance to spend money on interrogatories and depositions, and the net effect is that the case may dangle on the docket until it comes up for trial. The auto accident backlog becomes the real defense for the creditors' rights case, the defendant always hoping that something, whether an upswing in his fortunes or bankruptcy, will occur before the case comes to trial.

The only real cure for these cases I know is the creation of a fast track. In overwhelming number, these cases will take little or no time at all for disposition once they are reached. The various states have attempted to handle the smaller cases by the creation of small claims or municipal courts, but the charm of paying slowly does not lose its attractiveness as the higher figures are reached; indeed, it is the $50,000 or $100,000 defendant who may particularly want all the time he can get in the hope that his ship will come in. Some courts have experimented with short cause calendars, making special and expedited arrangements for cases not likely to take long, which leads to this *Recommendation:*

> 31. The law's delays are bad enough at best; but the waste is at its worst when parties are required to wait two or three years for one hour of a court's time. As soon as a case is at issue, either party should be entitled to ask that it be heard as a short cause. The court should then have some kind of investigative procedure to determine whether it is probable that the case can be swiftly disposed of, and such cases should be given a priority.

Bankruptcy procedure is itself in need of improvement, which is now under study by a special committee. At the same time, it may have some procedures well worth moving into civil practice. For all its limitations, bankruptcy procedure has a great deal of which to be proud. Many an important matter can come on for trial in a bankruptcy court within two or three weeks of its inception, and this may involve complex matters of great substance.

The federal courts have a practice of requiring reports on slow-moving matters, but this is particularly enforced in bankruptcy, where there must be reports on all matters pending more than eighteen months. The necessity of reporting does have a stimulating effect on completion of work, and most of the time the delay is due to delays in other courts or waiting for the Internal Revenue Service to process claims.

One type of bankruptcy jurisdiction is known as *summary,* a highly misleading term if it suggests some excessively brisk disposition of business. Although there is talk in the cases that bankruptcy matters can be disposed of on affidavit as distinguished from "full dress trial," this is not really true, because affidavit procedure is not much used. The accelerated procedures of the bankruptcy court revolve on the summary procedure plus Section 21A of the Bankruptcy Act, which permits the broadest kind of examination into acts, conduct, and property of the bankrupt. Bankruptcy procedure also requires that the bankrupt file, showing schedules or statements of affairs, and that he turn over his papers and records to the trustee, much as I would require in domestic relations matters.

I do not personally practice bankruptcy law and I am in doubt as to how these procedures differ from regular civil depositions and interrogatories. But clearly there ought to be examination and evaluation of these and the other bankruptcy procedures to determine whether they do have something to contribute to the civil practice. Any such inquiry ought to examine what it is that gives the bankruptcy practice the spirit of briskness, for although it is easy to obtain extensions to take depositions, conduct Section 21A examinations, or otherwise prepare for trial, it is extremely seldom, in the San Francisco area at least, that either bankruptcy specialist or nonspecialist attorneys ever request additional time. In other words, attorneys can and do proceed to trial quickly when the system is so organized.[28] These thoughts lead to this *Recommendation:*

32. Bankruptcy procedures should be critically reviewed to determine not merely whether they can be improved but whether, in the bankruptcy procedures, there are methods usefully transferable to the general civil practice.

CRIMINAL PROCEDURE

My prime focus of discussions here is civil procedure; criminal procedure is largely outside my competence. But there is an important interrelationship. Both the command of the Constitution and the demands of a sound system of justice on which it is based require that criminal matters be given the most expeditious possible attention. The accused cannot "enjoy the right to a speedy and public trial," which the Sixth Amendment guarantees to him, unless there is a court with time to try him. Hence, if a court has a specific number of divisions, given divisions will normally be designated as criminal; and otherwise, the criminal cases will be given a priority before judges handling other business as well.

Sticking to the simplest illustration, the question of whether there are four or five criminal divisions in a particular court may well depend upon the procedural efficiency with which all of the criminal divisions handle their work; and if the work can be done by four instead of five, the practical effect is to free one more division to handle civil cases. A dilatory criminal procedure thus does, in a real sense, delay civil procedure. In New York recently a heavy volume of criminal cases extinguished civil procedure altogether—on December 2, 1967, Justice Bernard Botein suspended all civil trials in the Bronx for at least the month of January in order to put all judges to work to reduce the mounting backlog of criminal cases. At the time, civil cases were facing an average delay of three years. Justice Botein wisely said that they would have to wait—it was the choice of "human rights over property rights."[29]

The whole matter of the courts and their proceedings has recently been the subject of a major report by the President's Commission on Law Enforcement and Administration of Justice, with a highly experienced Commission and an excellent staff. Chapter V of their report deals with the courts and with some matters of procedure; I shall largely defer to the experts with only a few observations on scattered matters.

There is a considerable parallelism of problems between the criminal and civil sides of the courts; indeed, if anything, the quantity burden on criminal procedures may be even worse than in the civil cases, particularly as to minor matters. On June 15, 1967, Chief Judge Felix Buoscio of the Chicago Traffic Court reported a backlog of 27,000 unserved traffic warrants, covering parking offenses for 1963, 1964, and 1965. As he sadly reported, "At the moment, we've only got twenty-nine men"; he advised that he would need at least eighty to eliminate the backlog.[30] Dean Edward L. Barrett, Jr., of the University of California Law School at Davis has discussed the mass production problem; a few of his figures will give the flavor of the matter. In 1963, the FBI reported 2,259,081 arrests for the so-called seven serious offenses, with a total of 4,437,786 arrests in areas covering a 127,000,000 population. In 1965, totals for the seven most serious crimes were 2,422,121, and the total arrests in a population base of 134,000,000 in 1965 was 4,995,047.[31] All trends, for crimes against the person and against property, are up, with New York and Chicago burglary and robbery crimes at least doubled or tripled since 1950.

In California in 1963, there were 700,000 adult arrests and 250,000 juvenile arrests. At that time there were 4,000,000 nonparking filings in criminal cases in the municipal and justice courts in California. In New York City, there were 3,374,000 similar traffic matters, of which 2,150,000 were parking. In California, during the year ending June, 1963, there were 7,700,000 filings in justice and municipal courts, one for each 2.3 of California's 18,000,000 people. New York had a ratio of 2.6 to its population.

These cases must be handled in squadrons. The defendants in Los Angeles on misdemeanor arraignments are crowded into the courtroom like passengers on a rush hour subway, and lined up in long lines down the corridor. In a Los Angeles court that handles 200 to 250 persons, drunks or alcoholics, a day and can run to 400, a judge must make all of his decisions within a few seconds on the basis of a glance at an information sheet and at the prisoner. The other minor criminal matters in Los Angeles, which run to around 130,000 a year, must average, for receiving pleas and imposing sentences, about a minute a case.[32]

It is the view of every experienced observer I know that mass handling of minor offenses increases disrespect for law, and thus feeds further violations of it. Putting aside every consideration of constitutional liberty, dignity, and human rights, and regarding the problem solely as one of administration, mass produced criminal justice increases the volume of law's problems. In 1963, Justice Tom Clark spoke to the National Association of Municipal Judges on the law enforcement problems created by dirty, crowded, smelly courtrooms, with judges shabby, inexperienced, and untrained.[33] One of the most experienced criminal defense lawyers in the West reports that jurors who themselves have had unhappy minor court experiences are particularly likely to be sympathetic with the prisoner accused in a more serious matter.

In the area of minor crimes, I cannot make any personal recommendations of value and am restricted to the thoughts of others. Dean Barrett has made his suggestions in the work cited. He would reduce the areas that are criminal, just as I would reduce the areas that are civil, by increasing medical, psychiatric, and other attention to matters of alcohol and drugs. He would also increase the number of criminal judges so that the cases can have individual treatment. If so, I would hope that the possible impact of the increased number of criminal courts would take the civil necessities into account.

A few other thoughts follow.

There can be a workable pretrial in criminal cases without sacrifice of individual rights. There should be a production of the names of all witnesses whom both sides intend to call, and the government should produce statements of its witnesses. At the present time, under the *Jencks* rule, when the witness appears, the defense regularly asks for copies of the statements. These are allowed with sufficient frequency to interrupt trials with short ten- or fifteen-minute recesses throughout the day. Delays of this sort could readily be eliminated by the practice suggested. All documents should be produced and admitted.

The pretrial procedure might well follow that recommended by a Ninth Circuit committee.[34] As the committee says, the pretrial should be held with the consent of the defendant, but the defendant may well be induced to wish to cooperate because any discovery at the pretrial is to be a two-way street discovery. As the committee says, "The government cannot be urged to reveal its entire case without cooperation on the part of the defendant in waiving foundation as to documentary evidence or otherwise cooperating in making the procedure one of mutual benefit to the parties."

Consideration is needed as to whether discovery, like the discovery in civil cases, would expedite criminal cases. Such discovery is now obtained in state practice by permitting extensive preliminary hearings, which themselves may unduly consume court time; a much stronger hand could be taken in shortening preliminary hearings if there were some other discovery device. Limited interrogatories might also be used. All of this relates to pretrial because, owing to the special limitations on criminal procedure and the importance of avoiding either delay or undue expense, experimentation under direct orders and supervision from pretrial conferences for a period of time might be desirable.

Defense motions are likely to crop up on the first day of trial, with a resultant waste of time for jurors who are being held on standby. These motions should be identified at pretrial and some may be scheduled for advance consideration.

Two special matters ought to be considered at pretrial. The first is whether the case is likely to have very peculiar or special legal questions; if so, some arrangement ought to be made to dispose of those before trial. To give an extreme example, after the *Miranda* case was remanded by the United States Supreme Court, it came back to trial court in Phoenix, Arizona, for a new trial. Because of the extraordinary interest and importance of the case, it was handled with great care by the court and by counsel on both sides. In consequence, there were approximately nine trial days spent on the trial, of which only about one-half day involved the actual taking of testimony before the jury. Had there been a pretrial procedure at which the various confession problems in the *Miranda* case had been able to be considered, there would have been no need to hold a jury in the wings for all that time.

To routinize this procedure, if the prosecution wishes to use a defendant's admissions or confessions, the prosecution should be required, prior to pretrial, to file a request for admission with regard to such confessions or admissions. If the defendant refuses to admit, then the prosecution should make a preliminary showing of admissibility of such statements at the pretrial.

The recent cases of *Brady v. Maryland*[35] and *Giles v. Maryland*[36] hold that in appropriate instances, and to prevent the suppression of evidence, the government must turn over its files. At a pretrial a judge could look at those files to determine whether there was any likelihood of application of the rule. He could also determine whether the materials suggested the prospect of any substantial evidentiary problems.

There can also be settlement on the criminal side. Judicial encouragement of reasonable plea bargaining can occur at this point.

In our region at least, the federal practice of impaneling the jury is far superior to the state practice. In our federal courts, the counsel are required to submit questions in writing, which the court will then present to the jury. On the state side, on the other hand, there may be extensive *voir dire* by the individual counsel. This results in the familiar abuse of counsel trying the case in the course of impaneling the jury. In one extreme instance, it took thirty days to get a jury into the box. In a typical case on the federal side, a jury is impaneled in from thirty minutes to an hour, whereas on the state side, the time is running from half a day to a day. The prospect of saving four to six hours on criminal cases is too attractive to be overlooked.

An unreasonable amount of court time is wasted on bills of particulars. The government uniformly seeks to tell the defendant as little as possible about the charge against him, and the defendant always wants to find out a great deal—often more than he is entitled to. This jockeying regularly takes court time on bills of particulars, a waste that has been almost entirely eliminated in civil cases. A rule should specify what has to be produced on request, and this should normally reach at least

1. The time of the offense.
2. The place or places involved.
3. The person or persons involved.
4. The means involved.
5. The extent or nature of the particular crime.

Minor misdemeanors in the federal courts should be heard by court commissioners and not by judges.*

The best way to avoid waste of time on review of convictions is to get them right in the first place. In each major community, one or more courts should be open twenty-four hours a day. It may be possible to have a single judge serve for both

---

* Something of this sort will be permitted under an Act passed in 1968, subject to rules and procedures established May 19, 1969 by the Supreme Court, 18 U.S.C. § 3401; Pub. L. No. 90-578, Federal Magistrates' Act, Oct. 17, 1968, 89 S. Ct. 3 (1969).

federal and state matters. The twenty-four-hour court would exist as a court of record, with a court reporter in attendance at all times, for the purpose of providing the following:

1. Immediate arraignments on all arrests, thereby reducing trial and appellate questions relating to illegal delay.
2. Issuance of search warrants and arrest warrants, featuring the court reporter's permanent record of the testimony upon which such warrants are based. (This should substantially reduce issues concerning searches and arrests without warrants and concerning the propriety of issuing the warrants.)
3. Immediate bail hearings.
4. Giving, and placing upon the record, the appropriate warnings under *Miranda v. Arizona* (again, a device that saves time by limiting issues on postarraignment confessions).

The twenty-four-hour court would avoid incarceration for purposes of investigation, thereby eliminating claims of abuse of process arising out of such techniques. It would eliminate large numbers of attacks on evidence, both at trial and at pretrial proceedings, arising out of illegally obtained search warrants and arrest warrants. It would reduce the area of dispute with regard to confessions and admissions.

The rules of evidence for criminal cases should be completely reviewed in the direction of simplicity. The other day in our jurisdiction, an experienced trial court sat on Saturday so as to speed along a first-degree murder case and release earlier a jury that was being kept sequestered, away from home and family, for the duration of the trial. Over two thirds of the day was lost because of friction over evidentiary matters. A system that is this tricky and time consuming to operate is not good.

Criminal cases are sufficiently more stylized than most civil cases to make possible both anticipation of the problems and prediction of the time involved with a much higher degree of accuracy. My criminal law partner, Mr. John Flynn, is one of the most experienced of western criminal lawyers. He reports that he is rarely off as much as half a day in estimating whether a criminal case will take one day, two days, or three. He says, however, that there is an immense difference in efficiency, based on the quantity of experience of the criminal law judges—the experienced judges are much faster than the novices. In areas with elective judiciaries where the principal publicity is likely to be in the criminal cases, most of the judges, not unreasonably, want a slice of it; and this requires some rotation. Some method needs to be found for utilizing experience where it exists and at the same time allowing some inexperienced judges to move into the work. For this purpose, uniform jury instructions in criminal cases should be available in every jurisdiction.

Although the criminal cases are in a high degree predictable as to amount of time, there is inevitably slippage of time between cases. I think that the individual calendar system is wholly incompatible with efficiency in the handling of these cases. Inevitably, some judges will be caught up and others will be behind, and particularly with the desire to speed criminal work, there ought always to be a way of shifting surplus cases to judges who are able to dispose of them swiftly.

One other device for economizing on time in criminal cases is to devise a new method of handling insanity defenses. Here I fail statistically; I do not know in how many criminal cases, either in a region or in the United States, the defense of insanity is raised, nor how much trial time is spent in exploring it. However, I include the subject here in the belief, first, that the existing system for handling insanity defenses is itself extremely poor regardless of time; and, second, that appreciable time economies are possible.

My thinking on this subject is dominated by the article of Professors Goldstein and Katz, *Abolish the Insanity Defense— Why Not?*[37] Insanity is regarded as a defense to a charge of crime because intent is a necessary ingredient of most crimes (the *mens rea*). It is assumed that if a person is insane he cannot have the intent and therefore he has not, in this sense, committed the crime; his insanity may at least be a mitigating excuse. As these writers say, there is no legislative report, no judicial opinion, no scholarly analysis that faces the question of "what need for an exception to criminal liability is being met and what objectives of the criminal law are being reinforced by the defense?" From the purely social standpoint, the insanity defense is not really a defense at all; it is or should be a device for determining restraint of the insane person. The general objectives of the criminal law—punishment, restraint, rehabilitation, or deterrence—will be served by making some determination as to what is to be done with the insane defendant. None of these purposes is served by acquitting him.

The matter has not been enough considered; but I think that the insanity defense should be abolished and that the mental condition of the defendant should become a factor for consideration in the sentencing. With this there should be a reconsideration of the entire concept of *mens rea* in criminal law, or, at the least, its extensive modification. In this view, the insanity issue would go entirely out of the jury proceedings. A defendant charged with crime could then put in all available defenses—alibi, self-defense, entrapment, or simply, not guilty. But he could not put in the defense of insanity. No psychiatrist would testify at the trial. If the defendant were found guilty, the issue would then become what to do with him. For this purpose, his mental condition would be of the highest relevance, and here medical testimony would be welcomed.*

This proposal is materially different from the bifurcated trial system currently allowed in California. That system provides for a jury trial first on the question of guilt or innocence, and then, whether before the same jury or a new one, a trial on the defense of insanity. The leading criticism is by Professors Louisell and Hazard, who conclude that the system does not work well.[38] As they explain, the California Special Crime Study Commission in a 1949 report concluded that the system was resulting in "duplication of time and effort" in California, and recommended its abandonment. On the other hand, the minority of that Commission recommended that the second proceeding be tried by the court without a jury.[39]

The discussion by Professors Louisell and Hazard, reporting experience and views in California and reporting the experience of other states, shows that the bifurcated system has both its supporters and its critics. Their report was made in 1961. My own state has just adopted its own variant of the California system, and current reports from the Los Angeles area are favorable. On criminal matters, I am off

---

* The general point of view expressed above gained support from a distinguished source later in 1968. See K. MENNINGER, THE CRIME OF PUNISHMENT, pp. 136–39 (The Viking Press, 1968). Dr. Menninger discusses separation of the issue of crime from its punishment and says, "the absurd 'insanity defense' [should] no longer be necessary or tolerated." He says that we should "exclude all psychiatrists from the court room." Id. at 138. The object should be to determine "whether this man is capable of living with the rest of us and refraining from his propensity to injure us." Id. at 137.

the line of my own direct experience, and therefore, with an exceptionally high degree of tentativeness, I make the following *Recommendations:*

33. A widespread pretrial system should be adopted in criminal cases covering discovery, *Jencks* problems, admission of documents, and anticipated legal issues. Defendants should not be required to participate, but the mutual advantages to both sides should be sufficiently great so that, in most cases, each will wish to do so.

34. Where possible, with due regard for training new judges, criminal cases should be heard by experienced criminal law judges, and should be administered on a master calendar system. Most judges will not have criminal law experience, and there should be special training programs to equip them for such work.

35. The defense of insanity should be abolished, and become relevant not to guilt or innocence, but rather to the sentence to be imposed or the treatment to be prescribed. Short of so lusty an amputation of existing practice, the bifurcated trial deserves further exploration in insanity cases.

ADMINISTRATION

In 1966, at the meeting of the American Law Institute, Chief Justice Warren recommended study of the use of computers. In 1967, when the Chief Justice came back to the Law Institute, he sadly reported,

Only a year ago I suggested that we should study the feasibility of the use of the computer in judicial administration. Since that time, the possibilities and potentialities of this mechanism have continued to increase in manifold ways. Yet we have not been able to progress beyond the talking stage about this.[40]

The procedure of the courts is more than the rules governing how the lawyers make ready or present their cases. It also covers how the files are kept, how the cases get into court, how the orders come out. It covers the whole distribution of business within the courthouse. In a large metropolitan center, this may be very substantial business. A few years ago, for example, Los Angeles had 102 Superior Court judges serving a population of 625 million people. There were 150,000 filings of new matters a year; 9,000 members of the bar dependent on the operation; 150,000 jurors examined each year; and a staff of 2,700 people. There was a total budget of $25,000,000, and the court was housed in 18 buildings scattered through a county larger than the states of Delaware and Rhode Island combined.[41] Today the number of judges authorized for Los Angeles County is 134, and the total number of filings for 1966–67 was 181,186.[42]

In a statewide system, there can be a maladjustment of work distribution between busy and slack sectors; in New York in the 1950's, 19 of the 62 counties had 80 per cent of all cases, and those 19 were badly in arrears. In 4 of the 10 judicial districts of the state, judges averaged fewer than 115 days of court a year, in one district the average was 78 days, and in the metropolitan areas, the average was 165 days. These poor balances were not merely among cities in the rural areas; Queens and Kings counties had the same number of pending cases, and yet one county had three times as many judges and administrative employees as the other.[43]

Clearly, under these circumstances, a minimal object ought to be centralized statewide court administration. There should be a central administrative office, operating under the direction of the state supreme court, which can move personnel around the state as needed. Such moves are not likely to be altogether pleasurable for the judges involved, and there must be power to give orders. This program, which is one of the prime objects of the American Judicature Society, requires skilled court administrators, or personnel to run the system. This is a new profession in the United States, and its practitioners are hard to come by.[44]

These problems and these suggestions for dealing with them are by now routine. The wave of the future is systems analysis and electronic data processing. Any business with the volume of the Los Angeles court system today would have computer processing. Yet in March, 1967, the *Journal of the American Judicature Society* reported that "The possibilities of electronic data processing in judicial administration are just beginning to be explored."[45]

This leads to the problem of how to make courtrooms function. The everlasting war has been between the master calendar and the individual assignment system. Some believe that the best results are obtained by assigning each case to a particular judge when the case is filed, so that each judge at any given moment has his own calendar, for which he alone is responsible. The protagonists of this school believe that this arrangement will permit the judges to manage their own work, study the cases in advance, conduct their own pretrials, and generally meet and face responsibility. The contrary view is that a court should be divided into sections, one for criminal work, one for probate, one for juvenile cases, one for civil cases. Cases should then be distributed among those judges as soon as the judges are ready. Enough cases are scheduled for any given day, on the basis of experience, so that if Division 65 gets spare time at 2:00 in the afternoon, something can be ready to go at 2:30. This plan clearly requires electronic devices, which offer the only way of keeping in touch with exactly what is happening in dozens and dozens of courtrooms at a time and of moving cases into the empty spots quickly. If time is not to be wasted, the old, "Hmm, let's-see-now" style of court administration has to go.

I believe that the master calendar system is far superior, and in the large areas imperative, if time is not to be wasted. Our own community has recently, in what seemed to me an odd step backward, moved away from a central calendar and back to individual assignments. The result has been that in the most current of the divisions, litigants must wait seven and a half months from the time they are ready until trial, whereas in the slowest division, they must wait nineteen months. It may be a denial of equal protection to the litigants to make so much depend on the luck of the draw. On the other hand, the master calendar system is incompatible with the device of having the trial judge hold his own pretrial, an activity that occurs an appreciable time before trial. I do not personally know how to solve this problem.

A recent discussion of systems analysis as applied to the courts begins with the appalling case of Charles Harling of Washington, D.C., who was arrested on a charge of armed robbery of items valued at $29.10. He pleaded not guilty and demanded a trial. One and a half years after his arrest, he was put on a thirty-minute alert in the United States District Court for the District of Columbia. This means that he was required to be present from 10:00 A.M. until 5:00 P.M. each working day until his case was called, with the lawyers and the witnesses expected to be present within thirty minutes of the summons. Harling spent three months in the courthouse waiting to be called. On the day that the error in respect to his trial was discovered, the presiding judge complained to the United States Attorney that four judges awaiting criminal cases had been given no criminal cases to try, although there were sixteen at the time on thirty-minute alerts.[46] Surely systems analysis can be usefully applied to the functioning of the courts in the District of Columbia.

The *Harling* case, while outlandish, is more colorful than symptomatic; any system will have some breakdowns, as the army recently discovered when it failed to give a man any duty for a year in San Francisco. I do not pretend to understand how modern electronic devices can improve judicial administration. The whole trouble is that lawyers generally do not understand; they are simply not trained or experienced in this direction. As a result, we run a big business without the devices other parts of society running big businesses would most certainly use. We must free ourselves of this blindness; quill pen court administration of course must go. We need all the help we can get, and we must aggressively look for it.*

There are other contemporary devices that could be used. As Dean Charles W. Joiner of Wayne State University Law School has said, depositions of persons who are going to be called as witnesses might well be put on video tape. Particularly where witnesses can be made available at trial only with expense and difficulty, he says, changes in existing court rules should "be made to permit the jury to view the tape in lieu of the witness." This would eliminate both the travel and waiting time for the witness and the cost of transporting the deposition. Dean Joiner adds,

---

* The Federal Judicial Center is giving prime attention to computer administration in 1968. An experiment with the handling of some sixteen thousand names of prospective jurors by computer will be in operation in 1969.

Today it is essential to bring all witnesses and parties together at one time and place to give evidence even though that time and place is not convenient for one or all. Tomorrow the testimony of each party and witness could be taken at his convenience and when all is in readiness the jury could be shown the tape of all the admissible evidence.[47]

This leads to my *Recommendation:*

36. Both the federal system and the separate states must utilize all available electronic devices to manage the flow of their work. The bar associations and judges should not wait for someone to come and sell them a machine or service; they should set out aggressively to learn and to apply new methods. At the present time substantial knowledge is beginning to be made available. Good intentions are not enough; we must get at it. Experiments should be conducted with film tapes of testimony.

THE FLYING SQUAD SYSTEM

In the preceding paragraphs, I have spoken of the goal of the American Judicature Society to promote centralized court administration for the states. We need something of the sort for the federal system, and this will be hard to obtain.

As was noted in Chapter I, there is, inescapably, a difference in the effectiveness of judges. As figures given earlier showed, the output range in my own county runs two and a half to one. I have cited examples of the occasional Super-judges of the federal system, such as Judge Wright, formerly of the District Court in New Orleans and now of the Court of Appeals in the District of Columbia, who had to be replaced by a small army, and Judge Kilkenny of Portland, who is constantly current, handles auto accident cases at the rate of one a day, and has a good deal of time to get to other districts. I would add Judge Hubert Will in Chicago.

To the extent that Superjudges are the product of special training, that training can be shared; I have spoken about a training program for judges. To the extent that they are the product of some extraordinary native genius, the quality can only be admired or feebly imitated. But what is important for the purposes of this discussion is that this is a random talent that may turn up anywhere and that may not be at the place at which it is most needed.

The Chief Justice of the United States, as head of the federal judiciary, should be able to move the most effective judges to the points at which they are most needed. In so doing, the work in the places from which the judges are taken must also be handled. For this purpose the federal judiciary should be expanded by perhaps twenty additional federal district judgeships, each of which is to be of the temporary variety. That is to say, the holder of the judgeship will have it for life, as the Constitution requires for all judges; but the seat itself will evaporate upon termination of his service. These appointments should be made by the President upon certification by the Chief Justice that he is moving a judge for at least a year's period from the district in which he was originally appointed. It is to be hoped that the President will make these temporary appointments with special consideration for extraordinary effectiveness and ability, so that when the judge who has been moved returns to his home area, his replacement will be a valuable addition to another bench if moved elsewhere. The Chief Justice would have the duty to use the slack thus created in the system to put some of the most effective judges in the country at the points where they can do the most good.

The suggestion obviously involves highly practical problems. For judges who are moved, there will be acute personal dislocations of housing, family relations, and schools for their children, and doubtless some will decline to accept the duty. On the other hand, some will willingly serve in the ranks, and the expense allowances for these federal judges should be so adjusted that none will suffer for having done so.

The system can work. A few years ago, by a very special arrangement, twenty-five federal judges were sent into the Brooklyn District, which was in an appalling state due to the age and illness of the judges. The special team swiftly made a major dent in the Brooklyn backlog.* There is limited exchange today through a special committee that is very useful.

Nonetheless, the country does not at the present time have any such basic system as is here suggested, and this is no accident. In 1922, Chief Justice Taft proposed a variation of this plan, suggesting that there be a total of eighteen district judges at large, two for each of the nine circuits of that time. These judges could be assigned to any district in the circuit and the Chief Justice could assign them to any district in the country. Taft, in appearing before the Senate in support of the legislation (which covered numerous other points as well), said, "The principle of this Bill is the executive prin-

---

* Brooklyn keeps needing crash programs. In 1968, under an energetic program undertaken by Chief Judge Joseph C. Zavatt, the criminal docket of 650 cases was reduced to 250 in a six-month period, and a new attack on the civil docket was beginning.

ciple of having some head to apply the judicial force at the strategic points where the arrears have so increased that it needs a mass of judges to get rid of them."[48]

The Taft proposal raised immense opposition, and although the rest of the bill passed, this portion was stricken. Senator Cummins, Chairman of the Senate Judiciary Committee, justified the plan on the floor of the Senate as one that would utilize "to the fullest extent the judicial force of the United States, so that we need not create more district judges than are necessary to perform the work." This led to the response by Senator Broussard of Louisiana that "I see now that it is proposed not only to add eighteen additional judges, but to shift them around and have men tried by judges who possibly are not altogether in sympathy with the ideas of the people over whom they are presiding."[49] In his view, it was "absolutely contrary to the principles of our government to assign a judge from a distant territory to preside over cases arising in another community."

Although much more was said on the point, this quotation gives the flavor of the opposition. In the 1920's, the concern was Prohibition. Wet areas feared that the Chief Justice might send hanging dry judges into their territories and shove an unpopular policy down the dampened throats of their people. Under the original Judiciary Act, and for most of the nineteenth century, Supreme Court Justices did go out from Washington to sit as trial judges, but this gave the critics no comfort. And there is some merit in the objection, which requires that it have some respect. The traveling judge, sent out from the seat of the government to enforce its tyranny, has been an evil figure at least since Lord George Jeffreys set out on the western circuit for the Bloody Assize in the reign of James II. Seventy-four hangings in Dorsetshire and two hundred thirty-three hanged, drawn, and quartered in Somersetshire, are a small part of the story told by Macaulay.[50]

Although I recognize the possibility of abuse, its prospect appears fanciful. Judges now can be shifted about in their circuits and, by a system of mutual consent between circuits, can be loaned from one to another. No abuses have developed. For those who regard federal officials as a cloud of locusts rather than the servants of a common government, an occasional "foreign" district judge cannot add much to the storm. Undoubtedly there are today those opposed to the racial policies of the contemporary law, who would have much the same fears concerning intrusion into their private domain that troubled some when Taft made the proposal in 1922. But the balance appears heavily in favor of the plan. The object should not be to make permanent transfers; if a district needs permanent new appointees, there should be appropriate legislation and appropriate appointments. But in case of illness, temporary backlogs, or the plain need for instruction by example, the old Taft plan, or my modification of it, or some other similar device to give the Chief Justice more effective personnel control is desirable. Hence, this *Recommendation:*

> 37. The Chief Justice of the United States should have the power to move judges, as needed, to various parts of the country. If this removal results in deprivation in areas from which the judges are taken, there should be appropriate authority to create, by the normal processes of appointment, up to twenty additional judgeships. The details of the plan are nonessential, but it is essential that the Chief Justice of the United States shall have the power to move his judicial firemen about sufficiently to put out (at least) the smaller fires.

Conclusion

In these chapters I have sought to demonstrate—

First, that American civil justice has broken down; the legal system fails to perform the tasks that may be expected of it.

Second, the collapse is now. It menaces the rights of our citizens to a determination of their disputes, and jeopardizes the capacity of commerce and industry for reasonable planning and action.

Third, the curve is down; the situation is getting worse.

Fourth, we have no generally accepted remedy. We do not even have a generally accepted program for discussion.

Fifth, our talents are required to develop a new agenda for discussion and for action. At this moment, the greatest need of this sector of constitutional government is imagination. We must be prepared to reconstruct the institutions of the law and remodel our lawyers and our judges, even our buildings. We must be prepared to change the substantive law altogether, in every reach, cutting it down to a size our groaning court system can handle. We must be prepared most radically to change our methods.

As specific suggestions, I have offered these recommendations for consideration:

1. Let us determine whether legal education can be so altered as to reduce dilatoriness in lawyers, and if so, how. If this can be done, does it conflict unduly with other values of legal education, and if so, can this conflict of values be adjusted?

2. Law schools generally should develop for all students comprehensive and meaningful programs on judicial administration.

3. We should reconsider legal education to determine whether, without the sacrifice of other important values, it is possible to make the graduates substantially more effective in the handling of cases, both in and out of the courtroom, to the end of increasing the efficiency of the legal system.

4. Judicial pay and prerequisites must be kept at least roughly equivalent to the income of good members of the bar. In some of the states, this will require a radical change.

5. Work should be done to devise a system for the measurement of the quality of judges in terms of effectiveness and merit. When such tools are devised, serious studies should be made of the various methods of selection of judges to determine whether in fact one method truly is better than another.

6. We should determine whether the office of trial judge should be a kind of civil service position, to which a person may progress by virtue of special training and examination; we should attempt to develop methods of deciding whether such a system would be as well suited to our needs as the more traditional alternatives.

7. The program of the National College of State Trial Judges is a great success and should be expanded into the federal system. It should be broadened, or duplicated in the states, so as to give all judges an effective opportunity for advanced education both in the substance and the adminis-

tration of their work; and the exposure to such programs should be recurrent in the course of the judge's career. This should be supplemented by traveling and local education as well.

8. Research now underway should be continued to determine the types of physical facilities most conducive to the speedy dispatch of court business. This will relate to computerized assignment systems, discussed in Chapter IV; but in this connection, consideration should be given to the use of televised assignment systems in large courthouses, after the fashion of flight information in airports.

9. The Federal Judicial Center plan, as adopted by the Congress should be activated on a large scale; and the companion National Court Assistance Act proposed by Senator Tydings should also be adopted.

10. "New measures must be devised to assure prompt relief to hundreds of thousands of automobile accident victims and to reduce court delays caused by the press of personal injury litigation. Remedial devices to accomplish these ends should be thoroughly explored, among them: 1. eliminating the fault principle in determining liability in most automobile accident personal injury cases; 2. the 'basic protection plan' whereby the first $10,000 of loss would be recovered on an insurance basis; and 3. the establishment of machinery for administrative compensation as in industrial accidents."

11. All rules or statutes governing procedure should be carefully analyzed to ensure that their application will not take undue court time or add to the cost of litigation. The presumption in favor of economy and speed is rebuttable where fairness is at stake, but it is a strong presumption all the same.

12. Like rules of procedure, substantive rules of law should be created with an eye to the administrative consequences of their creation and the cost of determining them.

13. Contrary to what I think is existing practice, every alteration of law ought to be seriously and scrupulously evaluated both in terms of its prime objectives and in terms of its litigation consequences. Complexities of marginal necessity should not be added to any branch of the law where the operation will be time consuming or costly. The makers of substantive law should be, and often are not, consciously and sensitively alert to the problems of procedural law.

14. The grounds of divorce throughout the United States should be considered to determine (a) whether their existence serves any socially useful purpose; and (b) whether controversies concerning them needlessly burden the administration of justice without serving any good end.

15. Property distribution in substantial divorce cases should be the subject of an auditor's report, and court time should not normally be taken to determine these questions. The enforcement of divorce orders ought to be completely reconsidered, eliminating the contempt remedy for alimony violations and substituting other creditor's remedies. Failures to comply with child support orders should result in automatic penalties where the husband fails to obtain a modification of the order.

16. The legislatures generally should eliminate or markedly diminish or restrict the mortgage system. A trust deed system operating largely outside the courts should be substituted in its place, both for efficiency and economy.

17. A study should be made by state insurance commissioners or by the industry's attorneys through a joint committee to determine the benefits and losses in terms of

speedier and easier judicial administration if insurance liquidations and receiverships were transferred to the federal court system.

18. Bonding laws on public works ought to be entirely reviewed. Priority disputes in particular should be eliminated by clear-cut lines as to rights, and small bonds, which are prolific litigation sponsors, ought to be eliminated entirely.

19. Mechanic's lien statutes, and all related legislation, should be reviewed and rewritten to achieve maximum clarity and simplicity.

20. (a) Vast areas of present legal work should be eliminated from the court system entirely; the automobile cases are the most likely candidate.

(b) Existing law should be expanded as needed; but always with a conscious judgment as to how the expansion will affect the operation of the court system that is to apply the new law.

(c) Existing substantive law should be reviewed to the end of seeking to make legal controversies not merely less frequent, but also smaller, by altering substantive law and eliminating from the individual cases as many decision points as we can.

21. Statewide and local judges' conferences should go over the minutiae of their own procedures to satisfy themselves inch by inch and step by step that they are operating as economically as they can, both in time and in overall costs to lawyers and clients as well as to taxpayers. It will be a rare judge who will not find at least one thing he can do more efficiently if there is a tight re-examination of every separate activity.

22. Procedure should be altered to permit conference-type trials or part trials in appropriate cases.

23. Rule 36 of the Rules of Civil Procedure, the admissions rule, should as a matter of standard practice be used in every case to put the cost of proof, including counsel fees, on the losing party wherever the issue is unreasonably disputed.

24. Rule 68 of the Rules of Civil Procedure should be revised to establish a system of demand by the claimant and offer by the defendant. Costs, including counsel fees, should be charged if the eventual determination of the case shows either that the demand was too high or the offer too low.

25. Close study should be given to the revising and enforcement of existing rules relating to pretrial conferences so as to increase the number of factual stipulations after the fashion of Tax Court practice.

26. An experiment should be undertaken to mediate money demand cases, using only nonjudicial personnel. The most obvious possibility is to have trained insurance adjusters representative of the court consult with both sides in auto accident cases to try to lead the parties to agreement.

27. In every case that admits of settlement, there should be a pretrial conference that has settlement as one of its prime aims. At such a conference all parties should be required, with the penalty of not being able to use any other information at the trial, to disclose every fact bearing on settlement. The court should then recommend a settlement figure and lead the discussion. The conference may best be held with the judge who will try the case, though this is not imperative. Rule 16 of the Rules of Civil Procedure should be amended accordingly.

28. At the pretrial conference, the judge should think of the case as a series of decision points or issues, the disposition of each of which will take courtroom time. It should be his

goal at this point to strip the case of as many decision points as can possibly be removed. He may be able to decide the whole case by summary judgment, and in so doing he should insist that the parties offer then and there whatever of substance they expect to have at trial that will show that there is a material fact worth trying. Applying this standard, if he cannot dispose of all of the issues of the case, he should then decide as many as he can to the end of reducing the scope of the trial as much as possible. He can preserve absolutely the right to try genuine issues of material fact without thereby suffering the trial of any nongenuine issues of immaterial fact.

29. Courts should seek to avoid hearing accounting cases a document at a time. In such matters, independent expert accountants should be appointed by the courts to make reports, and they should be entitled to proceed in the normal manner of accountants rather than by the procedures of court proof. Only the exceptions to their reports should require court procedures.

30. There should be one method of enforcing judgments and the distinctions as to the form of the process ought to be abolished. The process should reach assets of whatever nature, unless exempt, and regardless of who may hold the assets. There should be an elimination of all technical distinctions between garnishment, attachment, execution, creditor's bill, and similar devices. The process for enforcing judgments should be continuing in nature; the practice of successive garnishments of income by separate legal proceedings at regular intervals should be eliminated, and the garnishment should stand good until it is terminated by some appropriate order or by payment. There should be interstate enforcement of process. In the federal courts, one can in a simple way enforce in one state a judgment taken in another.

A similar arrangement should exist for the enforcement of judgments between sister states.

31. The law's delays are bad enough at best; but the waste is at its worst when parties are required to wait two or three years for one hour of a court's time. As soon as a case is at issue, either party should be entitled to ask that it be heard as a short cause. The court should then have some kind of investigative procedure to determine whether it is probable that the case can be swiftly disposed of, and such cases should be given a priority.

32. Bankruptcy procedures should be initially reviewed to determine not merely whether they can be improved but whether, in the bankruptcy procedures, there are methods usefully transferable to the general civil practice.

33. A widespread pretrial system should be adopted in criminal cases covering discovery, *Jencks* problems, admission of documents, and anticipated legal issues. Defendants should not be required to participate, but the mutual advantages to both sides should be sufficiently great so that, in most cases, each will wish to do so.

34. Where possible, with due regard for training new judges, criminal cases should be heard by experienced criminal law judges, and should be administered on a master calendar system. Most judges will not have criminal law experience, and there should be special training programs to equip them for such work.

35. The defense of insanity should be abolished, and become relevant not to guilt or innocence, but rather to the sentence to be imposed or the treatment to be prescribed. Short of so lusty an amputation of existing practice, the bifurcated trial deserves further exploration in insanity cases.

36. Both the federal system and the separate states must utilize all available electronic devices to manage the flow of

their work. The bar associations and judges should not wait for someone to come and sell them a machine or a service; they should set out aggressively to learn and to apply new methods. At the present time substantial knowledge is beginning to be made available. Good intentions are not enough; we must get at it. Experiments should be conducted with film tapes of testimony.

37. The Chief Justice of the United States should have the power to move judges, as needed, to various parts of the country. If this removal results in deprivation in areas from which the judges are taken, there should be appropriate authority to create, by the normal processes of appointment, up to twenty additional judgeships. The details of the plan are nonessential, but it is essential that the Chief Justice of the United States shall have the power to move his judicial firemen about sufficiently to put out at least the smaller fires.

These recommendations are meant either to encourage thought or action along lines already becoming familiar (the auto accident suggestions are far from new) or, perhaps, to stimulate new thought. But the suggestions are without pretension; any or all may be unsound without affecting a final recommendation that is the most urgent and the most practical I can offer.

I refer anew to a suggestion in the first chapter. We are told by Mr. George Kennan that on April 28, 1947, Secretary of State George Marshall returned from Europe. "He returned shaken by the realization of the seriousness and the urgency of the plight of Western Europe, where economic recovery had failed to proceed as expected and where something approaching total economic disintegration seemed now to be imminent. . . . We had already delayed too long. The hour was late. Time was running out. 'The patient,' as he put it in his radio address to the nation on the day of his return, 'is sinking while the doctors deliberate.' "

The Secretary summoned Kennan. "Something would have to be done. . . . He wished me to assemble a staff and address myself to this problem without delay. I had a limited time (I cannot remember whether it was ten days or two weeks; I remember only that it was brief) in which to give him my recommendations as to what he ought to do. He then added characteristically . . . that he had only one bit of advice for me: 'Avoid trivia.' "[1]

The result was the Marshall Plan, and the reconstruction of Western Europe.

Surely if by research, imagination, expenditure, and effort, we can reconstruct a foreign continent, we should by research, imagination, expenditure, and effort be able to reconstruct our own legal system. American law today most desperately needs a Marshall Plan; and to create it, we need precisely what the Secretary ordered, a period for a creative, fresh look.

The former Chief Justice of the United States can provide the leadership that Secretary Marshall gave. Warren led the Federal legal system as did no other man before him; he was in truth the first real Chief Justice of the United States. Some of his recently retired colleagues, such as Justice Clark, carry similar weight with the bar and the state courts.

And so I come to my final *Recommendation:*

38. A suitable organization should create an atmosphere, raise the funds, do what is necessary to permit, as soon as may be, a new national conference on the American legal system. Such a conference should be headed by Chief Justice Warren, with someone like Justice Clark in some mutually

satisfactory collaboration. I suggest no further individuals with two exceptions: the extraordinarily conscientious efforts of Senator Joseph Tydings of Maryland to find means of state and federal improvement suggest that he be counted in; and Congressman Emanuel Celler has similarly demonstrated his interest. But the former Chief Justice should establish his own staff and settle on his own participants.

It should be the function of this conference, avoiding trivia, to suggest proposals for the complete overhaul of the American legal system. I do not suggest that these proposals would be or should be immediately put into effect; just as Secretary Marshall's proposals had to go to the President, the Congress, and the country, so would the proposals of this conference.

It would be a crowning contribution to a lifetime's work if the former Chief Justice, who has been so powerful in establishing the country's twentieth century race relations program, its system of political representation, and its standards of criminal justice, might also lead the country toward a legal system reconstructed for the rest of this century. I recommend a Warren Commission for American Law.

References

CHAPTER I. THE PROBLEM: THE PIG
IN THE PARLOR

[1] Address by Chief Justice Earl Warren, 1958 Annual Meeting, American Bar Association, taken from Yager, *Justice Expedited*, 7 U.C.L.A. L. REV. 57 (1960).

[2] Address by Chief Justice Earl Warren, American Law Institute (1967), pamphlet.

[3] Banks, *The Crisis in the Courts*, FORTUNE, December, 1961.

[4] *Id.* at 7.

[5] *Crisis in the Federal Courts*, Hearings on S. 915 and H.R. 6111 Before the (Tydings) Subcomm. on the Improvements in the Judicial Machinery, Comm. on the Judiciary, 90th Cong., 1st Sess. at 438 (1967), hereafter identified in these notes as the *Tydings Hearings*.

[6] H. ZEISEL, H. KALVEN & B. BUCHHOLZ, DELAY IN THE COURT 206 (Little, Brown & Co., 1959).

[7] J. GROSSMAN, LAWYERS AND JUDGES (John Wiley & Sons, Inc. 1965), is the leading study. There have, inevitably, been exceptions to a good record; the ABA Committee (ineffectively) opposed a good appointment in Phoenix.

[8] 2 *supra.*

[9] Address by Justice Tom Clark to Arden House Conference, 49 J. AM. JUD. SOC'Y No. 1, 9 (1965).

[10] *Tydings Hearings* at 5.

[11] *Id.* at 11.

[12] *Id.* at 22, 23.

[13] *Id.* at 18.

[14] ". . . As a litigant I should dread a lawsuit beyond almost anything short of sickness and death." Address by L. Hand, 1921, reprinted in D. LOUISELL & G. HAZARD, CASES ON PLEADING AND PROCEDURE 1296, 1297 (Foundation Press 1962).

[15] Mimeographed Report of Special Committee of the Judicial Conference of the United States for meeting of March 30-31, 1967, p. 5; printed report, *Tydings Hearings* at 31. In the interest of brevity, these lectures do not go into appeals congestion. For a comprehensive analysis of this problem in the federal courts, see W. Shafroth, Statement, *Tydings Hearings* at 55-199; and for concise analysis of staff need, the statement of Judge Clement F. Haynsworth of the Fourth Circuit, *id.* at 215; Reports of the Director of the Administrative office of United States courts. Delays of five to six years after argument occur in the Alabama Supreme Court; Note, 21 ALA. L. REV. 150 (1968).

[16] New York Post, Mar. 16, 1967.

[17] Calif. Exec. Officer's Rept. 3 (1966).

[18] Computed by A. W. Saffert, Actuary, National Producers Life Insurance Company, from 1958 Commissioner's Standard Ordinary Table of Mortality.

[19] *Tydings Hearings* at 4.

[20] On Abraham Lincoln's pleadings and pleading problems, see numerous references in my LINCOLN AS A LAWYER (Ill. Univ. Press 1961).

[21] Reprinted at 35 F.R.D. 247 (1964).

[22] It may be added parenthetically that today, about sixty years later, conditions are improving in Missouri—of the first twenty-five cases in the most recent bound volume of SOUTH-WESTERN REPORTS, ten did not turn on points of practice or procedure or evidence or other rules of the game at all; eleven had such points in them, but were not controlled by them; and four were dominated by such questions.

[23] These activities were also spurred by M. STOREY, THE RE-FORM OF LEGAL PROCEDURE (Yale Univ. Press 1911); it is one of the sad notes of today that my own lectures of 1968 must echo so much of Pound and Storey.

[24] Recent work suggests many qualifications of these conclusions; see W. GLASER, PRETRIAL DISCOVERY (Russell Sage Foundation, Inc., 1968), done for Advisory Committee on Civil Procedure of the Judicial Conference and supervised by Prof. M. Rosenberg.

[25] See Frank, *Justice Tom Clark and Judicial Administration,* 46 TEX. L. REV. 5 (1967). In the lower federal courts, a principal successor to Judge Parker's position as an active reformer is Judge Alfred Murrah of the Tenth Circuit; for details of activities in which he has been involved, including notably pretrial, see *Tydings Hearings* at 311.

[26] Some of the Judicial Conference activities under the Warren leadership were: (1) The development of the HANDBOOK OF REC-OMMENDED PROCEDURES FOR THE TRIAL OF PROTRACTED CASES. In 1960, Presiding Judge Sylvester Ryan of the Southern District of New York, reported at least 350 potentially protracted cases there. Among the great cases is one with 18,000 pages of record; one with 45,000 pages; one with 70,000 pages; one with 4,600 exhibits; and one with 6,000 exhibits. (2) The disposition of the electrical antitrust cases. In 1962 there were 1,912 such cases involving 25,623 separate claims in 35 districts. For details, see the Murrah report, *Tydings Hearings* at 321. (3) An educational program, including seminars for new judges; sentencing institutes; programs for referees in bankruptcy; training programs for probation officers; training programs for court commissioners. The list is taken from mimeographed Report of Special Committee of the Judicial Conference for meeting of Mar. 30-31, 1967.

[27] Frank, *Justice Clark and Judicial Administration,* 46 TEX. L. REV. 5 (1967).

[28] THE COURTS, THE PUBLIC, AND THE LAW EXPLOSION, ch. II (H. Jones, ed.) (Prentice-Hall, Inc. 1965), hereafter cited as Arden House Report.

[29] *Id.* at 55.

[30] Wright, *The Federal Courts,* 52 A.B.A.J. 742 (1966).

[31] Letter from Charles Alan Wright to author, Aug. 19, 1966.

[32] Wright, *Procedural Reform,* 1 U. GA. L. REV. 563 (1967).

[33] And have; see my *For Maintaining Diversity Jurisdiction,* 73 YALE L. J. 7 (1963); and *Federal Diversity Jurisdiction,* 17 S.C. L. REV. (1965).

[34] THE COURTS, THE PUBLIC, AND THE LAW EXPLOSION (Prentice-Hall, Inc. 1965).

CHAPTER II. A NEW AGENDA

[1] G. KENNAN, MEMOIRS 326 (1967).

[2] *Id.* at 325.

[3] Joiner, *Lawyer Attitudes,* 50 J. AM. JUD. SOC'Y 23, 27 (1966).

[4] Cong. Rec. 2565 (Feb. 6, 1967).

[5] Mimeographed statement of Mr. Olney, p. 3.

[6] The plan is based on an excellent study by a committee headed by Supreme Court Justice Stanley Reed. Its first year budget is $537,000, of which $137,000 is for personnel and support, $250,000 is for education, and $150,000 is for research. For the Reed report, see *Tydings Hearings* at 42.

[7] Saari, *Financing Justice in America,* 50 J. AM. JUD. SOC'Y 296 (1967); the New York state budget for all courts is $120,-000,000 for 1967, New York State Bar News, Release, Apr. 7, 1967.

[8] Arden House Report 35.

[9] Literature on the pathological disruption of the time sense is collected in Wallace & Rabin, *Temporal Experience,* 57 PSYCHOLOGICAL BULLETIN 213, 223 (1960).

[10] Report of Chief Judge Thomas Clary, *Tydings Hearings* at 458, 462; Comment, 13 VILL. L. REV. 137 (1967).

[11] I have been advised in this regard by Dr. Sydney Smith, who deals with law and psychology at the Menninger Clinic, and Dr. Lee Meyerson of the Psychology Department at Arizona State University, who has reviewed the literature fairly closely.

[12] The great exception is Harvard. During the entire twenty-one-year tenure of Erwin Griswold, recently "retired" to the Solicitor Generalship, as Dean, every issue—168 of them—was on his desk by the tenth of the month.

[13] J. FRANK, MARBLE PALACE 139-40 (Alfred A. Knopf, Inc. 1958).

[14] Aronson & Gerard, *Beyond Parkinson's Law*, 3 JOURNAL OF PERSONALITY AND SOCIAL PSYCHOLOGY 336 (1966); refined and more fully developed by further experimentation in Aaronson & Landy, *Further Steps Beyond Parkinson's Law*, 3 JOUR. EX. SOC. PSYCH. 274 (1967).

[15] Ch. I, note 33 *supra*.

[16] H. ZEISEL, H. KALVEN & B. BUCHHOLZ, DELAY IN THE COURT, ch. XXIV (Little, Brown & Co. 1958).

[17] F. KLEIN & J. LEE, 2 SELECTED WRITINGS OF ARTHUR T. VANDERBILT 17 (Oceana Publications, Inc. 1965), hereafter cited as KLEIN, VANDERBILT.

[18] Reprinted at 21 U. MIAMI L. REV. 505 (1967).

[19] *Id.* at 544, 556.

[20] NEWSWEEK, June 19, 1967.

[21] KLEIN, VANDERBILT 24; Frank, *Why Not a Clinical Lawyer-School?*, 81 PA. L. REV. 911-23 (1933).

[22] G. HAZARD, RESEARCH IN CIVIL PROCEDURE 49, 56 (1963).

[23] 45 HARV. L. REV. 1, 10 (Dec. 14, 1967). The report says, "By the third year, apathy and eagerness to get out are the rule rather than the exception."

[24] Smith & Clifton, *Income of Lawyers*, 54 A.B.A.J. 51, 52 (1968).

[25] SELECTED READINGS JUDICIAL SELECTION AND TENURE (G. Winters, ed.), ch. I, M. Rosenberg (Am. Jud. Soc'y 1967).

[26] Unpublished remarks of Roger J. Traynor, Earl Warren Legal Center, University of California, Jan. 2, 1968. The supporting views are expressed by Mr. Sutro for the bar in Article 20 of SELECTED READINGS, *id.* at 154, also published at 51 J. AM. JUD. SOC'Y 128 (1967).

[27] This is briefly described in Kaplan, *Civil Procedure*, 9 BUFF. L. REV. 409, 413 (1960).

[28] Statement of Judge Alfred Murrah, *Tydings Hearings* at 314-15. Judge Murrah believes that, with time and experience, the National College has gone beyond the seminars.

[29] Report of the President's Commission on Law Enforcement, *The Challenge of Crime in a Free Society* 147 (G.P.O. 1967).

[30] Interview with Judge Irwin Cantor in Phoenix, Arizona, September, 1967.

[31] Green, *Logic vs. Tradition in Court Facility Design*, 50 J. AM. JUD. SOC'Y 220 (1967). This is a project of the Frank Lloyd Wright Foundation in Arizona, which accounts for my acquaintance with it. A leader in the field has been the Institute of Judicial Administration, which published *A Guide to the Construction and Renovation of Court Buildings* in 1958.

[32] For thoughtful analysis and illustration, see 50 J. AM. JUD. SOC'Y No. 3 (Oct.–Nov. 1966), a full issue on the subject, including articles by Judge Fort and W. H. Sobel, Chairman of the American Institute of Architects Committee on Courtrooms and Court Facilities; and for special attention to the vision problem, see Sim Van der Ryn, *Courtroom Design Criteria*, 52 J. AM. JUD. SOC'Y 150 (Nov. 1968).

[33] For an excellent introductory statement on the Tydings proposal, see CONG. REC. 2234-36, Feb. 20, 1967.

CHAPTER III. CUTTING THE LAW DOWN TO SIZE

[1] Unpublished opinion of the court.

[2] Judge Albert V. Bryan of the Fourth Circuit Court of Appeals has also observed the need of transferring Supreme Court efficiency; *Tydings Hearings* at 22.

[3] Hazard, *Rationing Justice*, 8. J. LAW & ECON. 1, 3 (1965) develops the social service thought rather more elegantly than in

my text above, concluding "Reasonable, decent and effective administration of justice is an irreduceably necessary social service and therefore outside the ordinary calculus of economic choices."

[4] The figures are well known and widely distributed; I take these from Moynihan, *Next: A New Auto Insurance Policy,* The N. Y. Times (Magazine) at 26, Aug. 27, 1967.

[5] These figures are taken from reports in the files of the Institute of Judicial Administration.

[6] I follow here the analysis of F. HARPER & F. JAMES, THE LAW OF TORTS, ch. 12 (Little, Brown & Co. 1956). There are important qualifications there which I wholly accept without needing to develop them in this text. The entire auto accident subject has been comprehensively but inconclusively reviewed by a California State Bar Committee; see Report, 40 CAL. BAR J. No. 2, 148 (1965).

[7] F. HARPER & F. JAMES, THE LAW OF TORTS, ch. 13 (Little, Brown & Co., 1956).

[8] J. MARSHALL, LAW AND PSYCHOLOGY IN CONFLICT (The Bobbs-Merrill Co. 1966). A close reading of the text will show that I have evaded generalizing about how often fault is obscure; this is because I have not seen statistics on this point.

[9] For purposes of these lectures, I am riding over the important differences among the various plans. The literature is extensive; the current reviews used in connection with the lectures were manuscripts of the papers delivered on "Basic Protection for the Traffic Victim" at the 18th Annual Advocacy Institute at the University of Michigan, May 10, 1967. A leading work is R. KEETON & J. O'CONNELL, BASIC PROTECTION FOR THE TRAFFIC VICTIM (Little, Brown & Co. 1965), which greatly influences but does not wholly persuade me; it contains a valuable survey of alternative plans in ch. 4. A comprehensive review of the status of all proposals is contained in a forthcoming essay by Professor F. Klein in New York University's SURVEY OF AMERICAN LAW.

[10] A. Ehrenzweig, "Full Aid" Insurance for the Traffic Victim (1954).

[11] This has resulted in the book, A. Conrad, et al., Automobile Accident Costs and Payments (1964).

[12] Columbia University Council, Report by the Committee to Study Compensation for Automobile Accidents (1932).

[13] See Institute of Continuing Legal Education, *Protection for the Traffic Victim: The Keeton-O'Connell Plan and Its Criticisms* (Institute for Continuing Legal Education, 1967).

[14] Kalven, *Plan's Philosophy Strikes at Heart of Tort Concept,* 3 Trial 35 (Oct.-Nov. 1967). Other relevant writings of Professor Kalven and of his colleague, Professor Walter Blum, are Public Law Perspectives on a Private Law Problem (Little, Brown & Co. 1965); and *The Empty Cabinet,* 34 U. Chic. L. Rev. 239 (1967).

[15] 8 for the Defense 73–80 (Dec. 1967).

[16] Kemper, *An Insurance Executive Looks at Proposed Changes,* 51 J. Am. Jud. Soc'y 168 (1967). This December 1967 issue of the Journal is devoted to this subject from various points of view. For a thoughtful criticism of the plan, see Professor W. Hold, the University of Texas, *Critique of Basic Protection* (1968 ms.); and see pamphlet, Defense Research Institute & Others, Justice in Court After the Accident (1968).

[17] Editorial, *id.* at 150.

[18] Kaplan, *Reflections on a Comparison of Systems,* 9 Buff. L. Rev. 409, 421 (1960). As a discerning critic who read a draft of these lectures put a similar thought, "We are getting farther and farther away from the mechanical approach to the law. To me, this is an inevitable maturing process. But like you, I'm not sure we can afford this luxury."

[19] For a leading discussion, see L. Hartz, Economic Policy and Democratic Thought, ch. IV, Sec. 4; ch. V; ch. VI, part 4 (Harv. Univ. Press 1948); and see J. Hurst, Law and Economic Growth (Harv. Univ. Press 1964) for numerous entries under

the index heading of "Separation of Powers," for illustrations particularly from the lumbering industry in the latter portion of the nineteenth and early twentieth centuries.

[20] I dissented from the Rule 23 change in the parts relevant to this discussion. I hope my colleagues in the enterprise will not feel that this is a needless continuation of a lost argument; but I am compelled to choose my examples in the areas of the familiar.

[21] A decision confirming these forebodings is *Eisen v. Carlisle & Jacquelin*, 391 F. 2d 555 (2d Cir. 1968), a suit by a claimant himself demanding $70, but presenting a class action allegedly for millions of persons. The evidence-taking procedures required by this Court of Appeals decision simply to determine whether the suit should go forward as a class action may be greater than the proof of the case itself if it is ever tried.

[22] Kripke, *Fixtures Under the Uniform Commercial Code*, 64 COLUM. L. REV. 44, 46 (1964).

[23] Hogan, *The Secured Party in Default Proceedings under the U.C.C.*, 47 MINN. L. REV. 205 (1962), clearly outlines the potential disputes that may arise; he concludes that more specific guidelines would not be desirable.

[24] See Felsenfeld, *Knowledge as a Factor in Determining Priorities under the Uniform Commercial Code*, 42 N.Y.U. L. REV. 246 (1967); II GILMORE, SECURITY INTERESTS IN PERSONAL PROPERTY, Sec. 34.2 (1965).

[25] 12 NY.2d 473, 191 N.E.2d 279 (1963).

[26] See *Comments on Babcock v. Jackson*, 63 COLUM. L. REV. 1212 (1963).

[27] *Id.* at 1243, 1246.

[28] The examples immediately following are taken from Proposed Official Draft, part 1, American Law Institute, RESTATEMENT (SECOND) OF THE LAW, CONFLICT OF LAWS (May 2, 1967).

[29] These examples are taken from tentative draft No. 9, American Law Institute, RESTATEMENT (SECOND) OF THE LAW, CONFLICT OF LAWS, Apr. 24, 1964. Dean Erwin Griswold has strongly

complained that this rule is "nonsense" for much the reason worried about in the text above; he is concerned that "every case is decided on its own facts" at an excessive cost to "predictability." See account of discussion edited by A. J. Keeffe, 54 A.B.A.J. 91, 92 (1968).

30 The refinements in this particular section strike me as only marginally useful; I wonder whether a simple rule which rests on the state of the misrepresentation would not do substantial justice with less burden on court time than will be spent in considering the variations.

31 The cases referred to in the preceding discussion are: *Tonsmeire v. Tonsmeire,* 281 Ala. 102, 199 So. 2d 645 (1967) (Alabama slander of chastity case); *Williams v. Shelton,* 125 F. Supp. 355 (N.D. Tenn. 1954) (the $25,000 case); *Good v. Johnson,* 366 Ill. App. 227, 83 N.E.2d 367 (1949) (award $500); *Holman v. Brady,* 233 F.2d 877 (9th Cir. 1956) (award $1,500); *Martin v. Johnson Publishing Co., Inc.,* 157 N.Y.S.2d 409 (1956) (award $3,000); *Shultz v. Shultz,* 224 Iowa 205, 275 N.W. 562 (1937) (award $3,000); *Freeman v. Busch Jewelry Co., Inc.,* 98 F. Supp. 963 (N.D. Ga. 1951) (award $5,000); and *Vigil v. Rice,* 74 N.M. 693, 397 P.2d 719 (1964) (award $2,000 compensatory damages and $5,00 punitive damages).

32 For discussion, see 3B Mertens, Law of Federal Income Taxation, Sec. 22.55 (1966 rev.).

33 For illustrative discussion of a few of the problems, see Mandell, *Twelve Month Liquidations and the Collapsibility of Real Estate Corporations,* 21 Inst. Fed. Tax 715 (N.Y. Univ. 1963).

34 Frank, *Obscenity: Some Problems of Values and the Use of Experts,* 41 Wash. L. Rev. 631, 670 (1966).

35 The phrase is taken from remarks of Professor Charles A. Wright, 8 Tex. L. Forum, No. 22, 4 (Dec. 8, 1967). See on the relation of the hearsay rule to court congestion, Smith, *The Hearsay Rule and the Docket Crisis,* 54 A.B.A.J. 231 (1968).

36 I have been advised on this subject by Professor Richard

Effland, Arizona State University, who has been involved in preparation of the draft.

[37] See G. OSBORNE, HANDBOOK ON THE LAW OF MORTGAGES 36 (West Pub. Co. 1951).

[38] Riesenfeld, *California Legislation Curbing Deficiency Judgments*, 48 CALIF. L. REV. 705, 728 (1960).

[39] For a hint of the wave of the future in which university discipline becomes a judicial matter, see *Soglin v. Kauffman*, No. 67-C-141, U.S. District Court, Western District of Wisconsin, Dec. 11, 1967, an opinion by Judge James E. Doyle, which opens wide this field, followed by his more comprehensive opinion and injunction of December 13, 1968.

CHAPTER IV. NEW MACHINERY FOR THE LAW

[1] "No scientist would think of basing a conclusion upon such data so presented. The court is not a scientific body. It is composed of one or more persons skilled in the law, skilled in the field which the dispute concerns, acting either alone or with a body of men not necessarily trained in investigation of any kind. Its final determination is binding only between the parties and their privies. It does not pronounce upon the facts for any purpose other than the adjustment of the controversy before it. Consequently there must be a recognition at the outset that nicely accurate results cannot be expected; that society and the litigants must be content with a rather rough approximation of what a scientist might demand." E. MORGAN, Foreword to MODEL CODE OF EVIDENCE 3-4 (1942).

[2] On the relation of legal and scientific methods to liberty, see Louisell & Williams, *The Parenchyma of the Law* (1960) as quoted in D. LOUISELL & G. HAZARD, CASES ON PLEADING AND PROCEDURE 1298-1302 (Foundation Press 1962).

[3] This is better said and illustrated in the address by Professor

Rosenberg, *The Adversary Proceeding in 1984,* to the National College of State Trial Judges in 1967.

[4] Address by Justice Tom Clark, 49 J. AM. JUR. SOC'Y No. 1 (June, 1965).

[5] Douglas, *Arizona's New Judicial Article,* 2 ARIZ. L. REV. 159, 161-62 (1960).

[6] This should not be read as an invitation to substitute impatience for the grace and real charm of a well-run courtroom. Every judge must keep in mind that, "The first signs of judicial taxidermy are impatience with trivial matters and the statement that his time is being wasted, for the secret of a judge's work is that 99 per cent of it is with trivial matters, and that none of them will shake the cosmos very much. But they are apt to shake the litigants gravely. It is only his power over people that makes them treat him as a demi-god, for government touches them more perceptibly in the courtroom than at any other point in their lives. The cosmos is made up of little quivers, and it is important that they be set in reasonable unison. Show me an impatient judge and I will call him a public nuisance to his face. Let him be quick, if he must be, but not unconcerned, ever. Worse than judicial error is to mishandle impatiently the small affairs of momentarily helpless people, and judges should be impeached for it." C. BOK, I TOO, NICODEMUS 4 (1946). (The passage is called to my attention by Federal Judge James E. Doyle of Wisconsin.)

[7] For very good citations and helpful discussion of this system, see Q. JOHNSTONE & D. HOPSON, LAWYERS AND THEIR WORK 64, 496-508 (The Bobbs-Merrill Co., Inc., 1967).

[8] See Note, *Use of Taxable Costs to Regulate the Conduct of Litigants,* 53 COLUM. L. REV. 78 (1953).

[9] See for example, Barton, *Payment into Court,* 34 N.Y. ST.B. J. 471 (1962); Geller, *Unreasonable Refusal to Settle and Calendar Congestion,* 34 N.Y.ST. B. J. 477 (1966); Note, *Deterring Unjustifiable Litigation by Imposing Substantial Costs,* 44 ILL. L. REV. 507 (1949).

[10] See generally, Finman, *The Request for Admissions,* 71 YALE L. J. 371 (1962).

[11] See S.B. No. 650, Mar. 3, 1965, California Legislature; the Bill was based on a memorandum of Judge Gumpert to the Committee on Additional Judges of the Superior Court of California, Dec. 30, 1964.

[12] Letter from Judge Gumpert to author, Nov. 30, 1967.

[13] Frank, *Pretrial Conferences and Discovery—Disclosure or Surprise,* INS. L. J. 661 (November, 1965).

[14] For some discussion showing that there remains room for surprise even with this stipulation procedure, see Mednick, *Pretrial Strategy in a Tax Case,* 22 N.Y.U. INST. ON FED. TAXATION 125, 131-34 (1964). I am indebted for help on the discussion of this phase of this matter to Judge William Fay of the Tax Court.

[15] This information is furnished by Mr. Randolph Caldwell, Jr., Clerk of the Tax Court.

[16]

Name	*Docket No.*	*Citation*	*Trial Time*
Kapel Goldstein and			
Tille Goldstein	94448	44 T.C. 284	4 hrs, 50 min.
Comtel Corporation	225-63	45 T.C. 294	4 hrs, 10 min.
John Town, Inc.	362-63	46 T.C. 107	2 hrs, 5 min.

[17] Statement of Judge Harvey M. Johnsen, Eighth Circuit Court of Appeals, *Tydings Hearings* at 29.

[18] For a comprehensive discussion, see the excellent work of A. Van Alstyne & H. Grossman, *California Pretrial and Settlement Procedures,* ch. 7 CAL. PRAC. HDBK. (1963).

[19] 162 F.2d 893 (2d Cir. 1947).

[20] Judge Learned Hand at 162 F.2d 903.

[21] For an excellent historical review, see R. Millar, CIVIL PROCEDURE OF THE TRIAL COURT IN HISTORICAL PERSPECTIVE 237 (Nat. Conf. Jud. Councils 1952); and for a clear statement of contemporary pros and cons, F. JAMES, JR., CIVIL PROCEDURE 230 (Little, Brown & Co. 1965).

[22] For citations, see C. WRIGHT, FEDERAL COURTS 387, part of a general discussion, 385-90 (West Pub. Co. 1963).

[23] C. Wright & H. Reasoner, Procedure—The Handmaid of Justice, Selected Essays of Judge Charles E. Clark 134-35 (West Pub. Co. 1965); and see Judge Clark's Essay *The Summary Judgment* at p. 18 of the same volume.

[24] I requested research on the utility of this motion by the office of the Administrator of the United States Courts under the direction of the reporter for the Advisory Committee on Civil Procedure. This research developed that in a small number of cases there was some function in the motion to dismiss, and I therefore have abandoned the proposal to abolish it, although I certainly do not intend to use it.

[25] There have in the past been proposals that a court might be able to direct summary judgment even though neither counsel had asked for it; I have previously opposed such proposals, but on more mature consideration, I very much doubt that I was right.

[26] 33 C.J.S. *Executions* 133.

[27] V. Countryman, Cases and Materials on Debtor and Creditor (Little, Brown & Co. 1964).

[28] I am indebted for the thoughts expressed in the text in relation to bankruptcy to Mr. Daniel R. Cowans, a referee in bankruptcy for the Northern District of California, who is widely regarded as outstanding. His own conviction of the transferability of bankruptcy procedures is strong argument for at least further study of the possibility.

[29] 158 N.Y.L.J. No. 10, p. 1 (Dec. 3, 1967).

[30] Judge Buoscio, unidentified newspaper clipping.

[31] Figures taken from Commission on Law Enforcement Report, ch. 2, 18-22.

[32] Figures are all taken from E. Barrett, Jr., *Criminal Justice: The Problem of Mass Production* in the Arden House Report.

[33] Frank, *Justice Clark and Judicial Administration,* 46 Tex. L. Rev. 5, 28 (1967). The leading force to upgrade traffic handling is the Traffic Court Program of the American Bar Association; for an account, see their publication Services Available (1967).

[34] See Report, 37 F.R.D. 95 (1967).

[35] 373 U.S. 83, 83 S. Ct. 1194, 10 L. Ed. 2d 215 (1963).

[36] 386 U.S. 66, 87 S. Ct. 793, 17 L. Ed. 2d 1747 (1967).

[37] Goldstein & Katz, 72 YALE L. J. 852 (1963). This proposal is beginning to take hold. Distinguished endorsements of the same approach are given by Chief Justice Weintraub of New Jersey, 49 AM. BAR ASSN. J. 1075 (1963), and in *United States v. Chandler*, 393 F.2d 920 (4th Cir. 1968).

[38] Louisell & Hazard, *Insanity as a Defense: The Bifurcated Trial*, 49 CALIF. L. REV. 805 (1961).

[39] Professors Louisell and Hazard feel that this raises a substantial constitutional question. I completely agree if the issue on the second hearing is guilt or innocence. On the other hand, I would not suppose the question so substantial if the issue is one of sentence. While there is authority suggesting that *mens rea* is a constitutionally required element of a crime, I am hard put to know why. Nonetheless, the defendant might have an advisory jury option on the second hearing without defeating the prime purpose of the suggestion.

[40] Address by Chief Justice Earl Warren to the American Law Institute, May 16, 1967.

[41] Address by Edward C. Gallas, Executive Office of the Superior Court of Los Angeles, included in NEW ANGLES IN COURT ADMINISTRATION (Inst. Jud. Admin. 1961).

[42] Major round numbers are civil, 40,000; criminal, 20,000; domestic relations, 42,000; juvenile, 28,000; and probate, 21,000.

[43] *Bad Housekeeping* (Assoc. of the Bar of the City of New York 1956).

[44] For details on the functions, qualifications and salaries of court administrators, see Information Sheet No. 34, American Judicature Society, July, 1966. There also needs to be a complete review of how much supporting personnel a judge can constructively use; Senator Tydings has listed this as a current area of study, *Tydings Hearings* at 5; and Judge John R. Brown of the Fifth Circuit makes a strong case for increased staff, *id.* at 217-21.

[45] 50 J. AM. JUD. SOC'Y 220 (March, 1967).

[46] Navarro & Taylor, *An Application of Systems Analysis,* 51 J. AM. JUD. SOC'Y 47 (Aug.-Sept., 1967); and for greater detail, their Statements, *Tydings Hearings* at 384-437.

[47] Unpublished remarks of Dean Joiner to the Iowa Academy of Trial Lawyers, Iowa City, Iowa, May 13, 1967.

[48] A. MASON, WILLIAM HOWARD TAFT 99 (Simon & Schuster 1964). Another possibility of emergency treatment for logjams is judges pro tempore, special appointments from the bar for short periods or even for particular cases. For some preliminary analysis of the problems, with local bar attitudes, see Judge H. Stevens on Judges Pro Tem, Arizona Weekly Gazette, Oct. 10, 1967, § 8 at 8.

[49] 62 CONG. REC. 4847 (1922).

[50] T. MACAULAY, 1 HISTORY OF ENGLAND 484, *et seq.*

CONCLUSION

[1] G. KENNAN, MEMOIRS 155-56 (Little, Brown & Co. 1967).

Index